LIGHTING THE WAY - A PARENT'S GUIDE TO WALKING WITH TEENS AND YOUNG ADULTS THROUGH SUBSTANCE USE AND MENTAL HEALTH CHALLENGES

Dedication

This book bears only one author's name, but it is the product of many hearts, hands, and voices that have supported me along the way.

To my remarkable, gracious, and courageous wife, Katherine, and to my lovely, brilliant, and endlessly delightful daughter, Luna — you are my heart, my foundation, my inspiration, and my reason for believing in the possibility of healing. To my parents, Michael and Thea, who were asked to learn how to parent a young adult in crisis without a roadmap, and who met that challenge with humility, strength, and unwavering love — your journey helped shape the heart of this book. To my long-time mentor, Wendy Caplan, whose wisdom and steady presence have guided both my clinical work and my growth as a human being. To my constant supporter, confidant, and friend, Benji Fleischer, whose belief in me has never wavered. To my Tuesday warriors, who have walked beside me, and held me up, through many of the most meaningful chapters of my life. And to Rachel Clark, and my friends and teammates at Searchlight Therapy, who live this work every day with compassion, integrity, and courage.

Most of all, I am grateful to the individuals and families I have had the privilege to work with over the years. Your courage in facing your darkest moments and your willingness to keep reaching for change have been my greatest privilege and my greatest teachings. This book exists because of the wisdom you have shared and the bravery you continue to show. Thank you for allowing me to walk alongside you.

Contents

Chapter 1

When Worry Turns to Fear

> **Sometimes the first sign of a storm is the change in the air, not the rain**

The shift often begins so quietly that you question whether it is even there. Your teenager or young adult sleeps later, laughs less, keeps their door closed a little longer. They stop mentioning names that once filled every sentence. Their eyes look tired; their answers come shorter. You tell yourself it is just part of growing up — hormones, independence, growing pains. But something in the air has changed.

In most families, the first stage of crisis isn't chaos; it is confusion. The ground moves subtly beneath your feet. One week your loved one is fine, the next they're withdrawn, irritable, or unrecognizable. You replay conversations in your head, searching for clues: *When did it start? Did I miss something?*

The Space Between Worry and Fear

Parents often describe this early stage as a tug-of-war between instinct and logic. Your gut whispers that something is wrong; your mind insists that it can't be. This is the space between worry and fear — the in-between where so many families live for months or even years. it is a space filled with rationalizations that may sound like comfort but feel like avoidance. You start making small bargains with yourself:

If their grades don't drop, it is fine.
If they're still seeing their friends, it can't be serious.
If they just make it through the semester, we'll be okay.

Each thought is a way of managing uncertainty — an effort to stay in control when control feels impossible.

What's happening inside, though, is more complex. Your nervous system tends to sense threat long before the conscious mind accepts it. That internal tension — the knowing-without-knowing — keeps parents on high alert, scanning for proof that their intuition is either right or wrong. Every sigh, every closed door, every late text becomes data to interpret. You may notice yourself oscillating between extremes: one day convinced that everything is fine, the next convinced it is falling apart. This emotional whiplash is exhausting. it is the nervous system trying to make sense of mixed signals.

The danger of the space between worry and fear is that it can stretch indefinitely. Many parents stay here not because they don't care, but because moving out of it means naming something painful — *My loved one might be struggling in a way I don't understand.* Naming it makes it real. So you gather evidence quietly: subtle changes in friends, new secrecy around the phone, shifts in mood or hygiene. You begin to track timelines in your mind — *When did that start? Has it been weeks? Months?* The desire to find certainty collides with the desire not to know.

This is where denial often hides — not in ignorance, but in love. Denial says, *maybe it is nothing. Maybe they just need time.* And sometimes, denial is even protective; it helps parents pace themselves, absorbing reality in doses they can manage. But if it lingers too long, it delays the chance for early support — the kind that prevents small problems from becoming crises. Clinically, this is the window of greatest opportunity. it is when intervention can be gentle, when conversations can be grounded in curiosity instead of confrontation. The earlier patterns are acknowledged, the less shame and secrecy take hold. Yet emotionally, this is also the hardest window to act within — because the evidence never feels definitive enough to justify action.

Parents often say later, "I wish I had trusted my gut." The gut — that quiet, persistent intuition — is not paranoia. it is the body's way of recognizing change. You don't need a diagnosis to validate concern. You only need curiosity and compassion to begin the conversation.

If you find yourself in this in-between space, start by observing without judgment. Keep a small mental note of changes — in energy, tone, behavior, connection. Ask gentle questions, not interrogations:

"You've seemed off lately. Is everything okay?"
"I've noticed you've been staying in your room more. Do you need some space, or would you like some company?"

Even if they roll their eyes or push you away, your calm attention communicates something powerful: *I see you, and I care enough to notice.*

The space between worry and fear is not failure; it is awareness awakening. it is the emotional threshold where love meets reality — where parents begin to understand that noticing is an act of courage, and asking is an act of love. Trust that instinct. it is the first light in the dark.

Recognizing Early Signs

Every young person's path looks different, but the early warning signs of substance use or emotional distress often appear in three overlapping domains: **behavioral, relational, and physical**.

Behavioral shifts may include:

-Noticeable changes in sleep patterns — staying up late, sleeping through the day.

-Declining motivation or interest in previously enjoyable activities.

-Sudden secrecy around phone, friends, or schedule.

-Unexplained need for money, or missing items in the house.

Relational changes often surface next:

-Irritability and defensiveness when asked routine questions.

-Withdrawing from family gatherings or long-standing friends.

-Increased conflict or volatility without clear reason.

Physical indicators can be subtle:

-Bloodshot eyes, persistent fatigue, or rapid weight fluctuations.

-Neglected hygiene.

-The smell of smoke, perfume, or incense used to mask odors.

No single sign confirms substance use or a co-occurring mental-health issue. But a pattern across these areas

— especially combined with isolation — warrants attention.

How Fear Shapes Perception

Fear invariably changes the way we see the world. It alters perception in ways that may feel subtle at first but soon become pervasive, shaping every interaction between parent and a loved one. When a loved one begins to struggle, fear quietly moves into the relationship like a third presence in the room — invisible but constant. It begins to color every glance, every silence, every choice. A slammed door no longer feels like teenage attitude; it feels like defiance. A missed text isn't just forgetfulness; it is danger. Even ordinary moments may begin to pulse with unease. Parents describe feeling like detectives in their own homes, searching for clues instead of connection, scanning every interaction for signs of what might be going on.

This transformation is not a moral failing or a lack of trust; it is biology. When fear takes hold, the brain's threat response — centered in the amygdala — becomes hyperactive. The body enters a state of readiness, flooded with adrenaline and cortisol, prepared to react. The logical and reflective parts of the brain quiet down, while the instinctual parts take over. You start seeing everything through a survival lens, interpreting your loved one's behavior not as communication but as potential danger. The nervous system becomes the narrator, and its story is one of vigilance.

In this state, love can begin to look like control. The parent who checks the phone, stays up until the car pulls in, or rehearses every possible crisis scenario isn't acting out of distrust but of devotion. Fear is love in its most protective form — but when it becomes the only form, it overshadows connection. What begins as an effort to prevent harm can inadvertently create distance. The more a parent watches, the more the loved one feels watched but not "seen". The more a parent questions, the more the loved one retreats. Fear, trying to keep the relationship close, often ends up pushing it further away.

Clinically, we often describe this cycle as a system of co-regulated anxiety — two nervous systems responding to each other's alarms. A parent's fear triggers the loved one's defensiveness, which in turn heightens the parent's vigilance. The result is a loop of reactivity: one person's tightening fuels the others. The home becomes a place where everyone is bracing for something.

It helps to remember that fear narrows vision. It takes the vastness of who your loved one is — their complexity, their humor, their still-developing identity — and reduces it to a single, frightening possibility. it is as if the camera lens zooms in too far, cutting off the rest of the frame. What once felt nuanced becomes black and white, safe or unsafe, okay or not okay. In that narrowed focus, the richness of the relationship fades, replaced by constant scanning. Parents begin to mistake control for awareness and vigilance for care.

One of the hardest but most healing steps is learning to notice when fear has taken the wheel. When you feel your body tightening — your heart speeding, your jaw clenching, your breath shortening — that's your signal. Before responding, pause. Instead of asking, *what is my loved one doing right now?* ask, *what am I feeling right now?* The first question looks outward for control; the second invites inward reflection. This single shift usually interrupts the spiral of reactivity long enough to bring curiosity back into the room.

In that pause, you might discover that beneath your frustration is sadness, or beneath your anger is helplessness. You might realize that what you fear most is not your loved one's choices, but your inability to protect them from pain. Awareness does not erase fear, but it softens its grip. It widens your perspective again, allowing both you and your loved one to breathe.

Fear is not the enemy. Frequently, it is evidence of deep love — the body's alarm bell that someone precious is at risk. But when fear becomes the only lens through which we see our loved ones, it invariably distorts reality. It replaces empathy with suspicion and turns virtually every interaction into a test. By learning to slow down and identify what's happening inside of you, you begin to separate observation from interpretation. "They came home late" is an observation. "They must be using substances" is an interpretation. The first allows space for conversation; the second shuts it down.

Over time, parents who learn to recognize fear as a signal rather than a truth begin to reclaim their calm. They start to see that not every silence is a crisis, not every closed door is rejection, not every mistake is relapse. The nervous system settles, and perspective returns. As perspective widens, so does compassion — for your loved one, and for yourself.

Curiosity is an antidote to fear. Where fear asks, *what's wrong?* curiosity asks, *what's happening?* The former assumes danger; the latter invites understanding. When curiosity returns, the relationship is ready to heal. You can look at your loved one again and see more than symptoms — you can see the whole person: still growing, still learning, still reachable.

Fear may narrow your vision, but love, when paired with awareness, restores it. Each time you pause, breathe, and choose reflection over reaction, you are positioned to reclaim a bit of that clarity. You teach your loved one that home can still be safe — not because everything is under control, but because connection remains. And in families navigating the uncertainty of mental health and recovery, that connection is the most protective force of all.

Why Denial Makes Sense

Parents often judge themselves harshly for "not seeing it sooner." In the quiet moments after a diagnosis, an intervention, or a crisis, many look back and wonder how they missed the signs. They replay conversations, notice memories differently, and ask themselves why they didn't act earlier. But denial isn't ignorance — it is protection. The human brain is remarkably skilled at keeping unbearable realities at a distance until we're ready to face them. it is not that you didn't care; it is that you cared so much that the truth felt too heavy to hold.

Denial is one of the mind's oldest defense mechanisms. It does not erase facts — it filters them. It takes overwhelming information and packages it in smaller, more manageable pieces. It lets you believe your loved one is "just stressed," "just experimenting," or "just going through a phase," because the alternative feels too frightening to name. The idea that your loved one might be struggling with addiction, depression, or both can shatter the story you've told yourself about your family, about safety, and about who your loved one is supposed to be. Denial shields you from that shock until your heart is strong enough to bear it.

From a psychological perspective, denial often serves a developmental purpose. It creates an emotional buffer between awareness and acceptance — a waiting room where the psyche gathers its strength. it is why parents often begin by minimizing or rationalizing signs of trouble: *They're just tired from school,* or *everyone drinks in college,* or *this is what independence looks like.* These thoughts aren't delusions; they're attempts to regulate the unbearable. They are, in essence, the nervous system saying, *I need more time to integrate what I know.*

In family systems work, we see denial as part of the natural rhythm of change. Families rarely move from ignorance to action in one step. There's a gradual unfolding — suspicion, hesitation, disbelief, partial acknowledgment, and finally, courage. Each step has its own emotional logic. Denial isn't a refusal to see; it is the body's way of pacing exposure to pain. It buys time for the heart to catch up to reality.

There's also a hidden tenderness in denial: it is an act of hope. To minimize a loved one's symptoms, to find alternate explanations, is, in its own way, to keep believing in their strength. Denial often says, *they'll figure it out. They just need space. They'll come back to themselves.* it is not foolish optimism — it is love trying to protect both of you from despair. The problem is not that parents hope; it is that hope morphs into avoidance. When denial lingers too long, it begins to isolate. The parent may start to feel the dissonance between what they know and what they can admit. They may avoid certain friends or family members, fearing judgment or unsolicited advice. They might even downplay their concerns to professionals, speaking in cautious, softened phrases: "we have just noticed some changes lately," or "it is probably nothing serious." The desire to stay in control can make it hard to ask for help, and the longer denial lasts, the harder it becomes to break.

But there's another way to approach denial — not as a barrier to truth, but as a threshold to courage. The goal isn't to eliminate denial but to move through it gently. Naming it is the first act of bravery: *I don't want this to be true, but I'm willing to look.* That sentence captures the essence of healthy acknowledgment — honesty without collapse. It allows space for grief and agency to coexist.

The moment a parent names what they fear is often the moment the healing begins. It does not mean everything is fixed or even clear. It means that you have stepped out of the fog and into the light, however dim it may be. In that light, you can begin to ask new questions: *What's happening? What kind of support might help? Who can guide us through this?*

Moving through denial requires compassion for yourself. You were protecting your heart the best way you knew how. Shame has no place here. In fact, shame often keeps denial in place — it says, *If I admit this, it means I failed.* But acknowledgment isn't failure; it is love growing stronger. it is a parent choosing truth not because it is comfortable, but because it is necessary for healing.

If you find yourself standing at the edge of recognition, take your time. The journey out of denial does not have to be sudden. You can begin by simply saying to yourself, *something does not feel right, and I'm ready to understand why.* Even that small statement can open the door to help, connection, and change.

Denial, paradoxically, is often a parent's first act of care — the mind's attempt to protect love from breaking. But courage is what transforms that care into healing. When you are ready to look, to name what is true, you give your family the greatest gift: the chance to begin again, together, in honesty.

Understanding What's Beneath the Behavior

Substance use in adolescents and young adults rarely exists in isolation. It does not appear out of nowhere or happen in a vacuum. Beneath virtually every behavior — the drinking, skipping school or work, the sudden outbursts, the long silences — there is usually an attempt to manage something unbearable. For some young people, it is anxiety that feels constant and undefined. For others, it is a deep loneliness that social media or friendship cannot seem to fix. Sometimes it is trauma — not only from obvious events, but from the slow accumulation of stress, perfectionism, or emotional disconnection. Substance use becomes, in a sense, a language. It speaks what words cannot.

Parents often see only the surface — the lies, the mood swings, the impulsivity — and understandably, they react to what's visible. They ground, they set curfews, they search for explanations, desperate to regain control. Yet underneath those behaviors is almost always a nervous system in distress, a young person trying to soothe themselves in the only way they know how. When we focus solely on the behavior, we risk missing the message underneath: *Something hurts, and I don't know how to say it.*

In the early stages, the task is not to fix or punish, but to listen beneath. Listening beneath is not passive; it is an active form of empathy. It asks parents to look at their loved one not as a problem to be solved, but as a person whose behavior is telling a story about their pain. This requires slowing down enough to see beyond the surface, to ask *what is this behavior protecting them from?* rather than *what is it doing to me?*

When we reframe behavior as communication, the meaning begins to shift. A slammed door might not be defiance; it might be exhaustion. Withdrawal might not be rejection; it might be shame. Anger might not be aggression; it might be fear. Adolescents, especially those navigating substance use or mental health challenges, often lack the words to describe what they feel. Developmentally, their brains are still learning to link emotion to expression. Substances, risky behavior, and defiance often fill that gap — quick ways to escape or distract from discomfort.

For parents, this can feel both painful and confusing. You may find yourself wondering, *why would they choose something that hurts them?* The truth is that very few young people start using substances with the intention of self-destruction. They start because it works — at least at first. It numbs the worry, quiets the mind, fills the emptiness, or gives them a fleeting sense of belonging. In clinical terms, it is a maladaptive coping mechanism; in human terms, it is relief. Understanding that does not mean condoning the behavior — it means approaching it with compassion rather than condemnation.

The shift from control to curiosity is subtle but profound. Instead of "What's wrong with you?" we begin to ask, "What happened to you?" or even, "What's happening inside you?" That language opens doors instead of closing them. It tells your loved one that you're more interested in their experience than their performance, more invested in understanding than in punishment.

Listening beneath requires emotional steadiness. When your loved one lashes out, shuts down, or lies, your instinct may be to confront or correct — to make them see reason. But reason seldom works when someone's nervous system is in survival mode. What they need first is safety, not solutions. Safety does not mean agreeing with or excusing harmful choices; it means creating an emotional environment where truth can be spoken without immediate retribution. When young people feel seen rather than judged, their defenses soften. They begin to risk honesty.

Even small moments of attunement can make a difference. When you notice fatigue behind sarcasm, sadness behind irritability, or fear behind anger, reflect it gently back:

"You seem tired lately; is something weighing on you?" "You've been quiet today — are you okay, or do you need some space?"

"I get that you're angry. Sometimes anger is easier to show than fear. Which one are you feeling right now?"

These questions don't demand confession. They signal presence. They tell your loved one that you can handle the truth, even if it is messy or incomplete.

For many parents, this kind of listening feels counter-intuitive. They worry that empathy means letting go of accountability, that compassion might encourage the very behaviors they're trying to stop. Empathy and account-ability can often be considered partners. You can hold firm boundaries while still holding your loved one's humanity. You can say, "I don't approve of this choice, but I understand what you're trying to manage." That dual message — love and limit — is what ultimately helps young people feel safe enough to change.

Understanding what's beneath the behavior does not excuse harm, but it humanizes it. It replaces the question *"How do I stop this?"* with *"How do we heal what's driving it?"* It usually moves the conversation from behavior management to emotional connection — from control to compassion. If you remember nothing else, remember this: your loved one's behavior is a form of communication. You may not like the message, but it is still a message. The more you listen beneath, the more likely you are to hear the truth that lives beneath the noise.

Even a simple statement — "You don't seem like yourself lately; I'm here if you need to talk" — can be enough. Those words say, *I'm steady. I'm not going anywhere. I see the pain, even if you can't name it yet.* That's how healing can begin — not by trying to fix but seeing.

Turning Observation into Action

Once worry shifts toward concern, the next step is quiet inquiry.

Document what you observe over time. Patterns reveal truths that isolated incidents conceal.

Choose timing wisely. Avoid interrogating in moments of conflict or intoxication. Wait for calm.

Lead with empathy. "I've noticed you seem more tired lately — how are you doing?" is far more effective than "What's going on with you?"

Seek consultation early. Talking with a pediatrician, therapist, or school counselor does not mean you're labeling your loved one; it means you're gathering information.

Early intervention often prevents escalation. Many families delay reaching out because they fear judgment or overreaction. But professional guidance is most effective before crisis sets in.

Reflection & Awareness

1. **Notice the air before the storm.** Write down subtle shifts in your loved one's behavior over a two-week period without interpreting them. Observation precedes understanding.
2. **Track your own emotions.** Which moments spike anxiety or defensiveness in you? Awareness of your body's signals prevents reactive communication.
3. **Replace interrogation with curiosity.** Practice beginning statements with "I've noticed…" or "I wonder if…" instead of "Why are you…?"
4. **Reach outward, not inward.** Ask for professional or peer support early. Early connection reduces later crisis.

Closing Thought

Every parent begins this journey with the same wish: to keep their loved one safe. That wish is ancient, instinctive, and pure — the quiet heartbeat beneath every decision, every sleepless night, every anxious breath. From the moment you first held your loved one, safety became your compass. When something begins to feel off — when your intuition whispers that danger might be near — it is only natural to tighten your grip. You want to protect, to control, to fix.

But safety, as it turns out, begins somewhere else. It does not start with control; it starts with awareness — the willingness to see clearly, even when the truth is uncomfortable. Awareness asks more courage of you than control ever will. Control offers the illusion of certainty: *If I just do the right thing, if I watch closely enough, I can prevent this.* Awareness, by contrast, asks you to stand in uncertainty yet remain open. It invites you to see your loved one not as a collection of problems to manage, but as a human being in pain, deserving of patience and understanding.

When the storm comes — and it often does — it does not mean you failed. It means that life has entered a chapter you didn't choose but must now learn to navigate. It means that your loved one's path to healing has begun in a way you may not yet recognize. The storm is not punishment; it is transformation in motion. It strips away illusions, but it also reveals strength — yours and theirs.

Many parents reach this stage and say, "I just want things to go back to normal." But "normal" is often what kept the pain invisible. The goal isn't to return to what was; it is to move toward what can be — a family grounded in honesty, empathy, and resilience. The storm may scatter what you once knew, but it also clears the ground for new growth.

Learning to stand in the wind is an act of quiet bravery. It means finding steadiness inside yourself even as the world around you shakes. It means breathing when you want to panic, listening when you want to lecture, and trusting that connection — not control — is the truest form of safety you can offer. Sometimes standing in the wind looks like saying less and noticing more. Sometimes it looks like asking for help. And sometimes it is simply holding your loved one's gaze without turning away, even when both of you are afraid.

Awareness is not passive; it is the foundation of every healthy response that will follow. it is what allows you to recognize patterns, to act early, to seek guidance without shame. it is what helps you remember that you are not alone — that countless families have stood in this same storm and learned, over time, how to find their footing again.

If you take only one thing from this chapter, let it be this: love and fear can coexist, but awareness is what keeps love in charge. Fear will urge you to react, to tighten, to control. Love, informed by awareness, will help you stay present, to witness, to endure.

Your family's story is not over. The winds may rise, the sky may darken, but the light — the same light that has guided countless parents through uncertainty — still shines within you. And as you learn to stand in the wind, you'll discover something extraordinary: you are stronger, wiser, and more capable than fear ever allowed you to believe.

That is where real safety begins.

Chapter 2

The Myths That Keep Us Stuck

> **It is easier to believe a comforting lie than to face a painful truth**

When a family first encounters the reality of a loved one's substance use or emotional distress, a common reaction is disbelief. We reach for explanations that make sense of chaos: *it is just a phase. All teenagers experiment. They're hanging out with the wrong crowd. We raised them well — this can't be happening here.*

These beliefs are not rooted in ignorance. They invariably represent hope wearing the mask of logic. They can serve to protect us from panic by offering a story we can live with — at least for a while. But over time, these myths become walls between family members and the help they need. Families seldom get stuck because they don't care. They tend to get stuck because the myths surrounding substance use and mental health are loud, persistent, and socially reinforced.

Myth 1: "This Is Just a Phase."

it is comforting to believe that adolescence explains everything. After all, teenagers are supposed to be moody, impulsive, unpredictable. They test limits, crave independence, and swing between confidence and collapse. Developmentally, this is part of the process — for most, adolescence is a time of neurological development, when emotions grow faster than regulation can keep up. When parents observe irritability, withdrawal, or sudden changes, it is natural to think, *this must be normal.* And sometimes, it is. Many teens move through periods of restlessness or rebellion and emerge with greater maturity. But sometimes, the changes don't fade. They persist, intensify, or begin to interfere with daily life. Grades drop. Sleep patterns shift. Friend groups change. Once-familiar routines start to dissolve. Parents sense that something deeper is happening — yet the comfort of the phrase *"just a phase"* lingers like a soft denial. It buys time. It soothes fear. It allows the heart to breathe for a little longer before confronting what might be true.

Substance use or emotional distress often begins quietly, in ways that can easily masquerade as normal adolescent experimentation. It does not always look like the movies — there's rarely a single dramatic turning point. More often, it begins with small escapes: vaping to calm nerves, having a drink at a party to feel less awkward, isolating in a bedroom to avoid social pressure, gaming until dawn to silence anxiety, etc. These behaviors are not evidence of weakness or rebellion; they're attempts at regulation — clumsy, temporary ways of managing emotions that feel too big or too painful.

What starts as coping can quietly evolve into dependence. The brain, still under construction during adolescence and early adulthood, learns quickly. When it discovers a reliable way to escape discomfort, it builds pathways around that relief. Behavior becomes not just a choice, but a habit — sometimes even a necessity. By the time parents notice, their loved one may already feel trapped in a cycle they can't easily explain or stop.

That's why recognizing the difference between a phase and a pattern matters. A phase inherently has movement — it rises and falls, leaving room for growth. A pattern has repetition — the same struggle returning in slightly different forms. Distinguishing the two does not require panic or punishment; it requires curiosity without judgment. Instead of assuming *"this will pass,"* ask, *"what purpose might this serve?"* That question changes everything. It shifts the focus from behavior to need, from surface to depth. Every behavior, even the destructive ones, serves a purpose — to numb pain, to belong, to feel control, to escape uncertainty. When we see behavior as communication, we start to decode the language of distress rather than react to it.

Parents often resist this idea at first. It can feel counterintuitive to look for meaning behind something that feels unacceptable or frightening. But understanding the "why" does not mean excusing the "what." It means addressing the root rather than the symptom. If a young person is vaping, what anxiety might they be calming? If they're isolating, what social fear are they avoiding? If they're drinking, what emotional pain are they trying to mute? Curiosity does not condone — it connects. The challenge is emotional. Curiosity is hard to access when fear is high. Parents understandably want to intervene quickly, to stop the spiral before it worsens. But rushing into correction without comprehension often drives behavior underground. Teens, sensing judgment, become secretive. The more they hide, the more parents tend to worry. It becomes a dance of distance — both sides protecting themselves from the other's disappointment.

Breaking that pattern begins with pausing before labeling. When you notice changes in your loved one — more irritability, less eye contact, and withdrawal from old friends — resist the urge to decide what it means. Instead, observe. Reflect. Ask gentle questions. Even a simple comment like, "I notice you're doing things differently," invites dialogue without accusation. You may not get an answer right away, but you've opened a door that says, *I'm paying attention, and I care.*

Phases and patterns can overlap. What begins as a developmental phase can develop unhealthy coping mechanisms if it goes unnoticed or unsupported. The difference often lies in duration and impact: how long the change lasts, and how much it disrupts daily life. A week of moodiness is probably adolescence; months of withdrawal, isolation, or secrecy signal something deeper. When parents allow curiosity to replace assumption, they start to see their loved one with new eyes. They notice that irritability may be fatigue, that apathy may mask hopelessness, that rebellion may hide fear. Beneath every behavior is a story, and that story is always worth hearing.

"This is just a phase" is a comforting sentence, but comfort isn't always the same as care. True care means looking — gently, bravely — at what lies beneath the surface. It means trusting your intuition when something feels off and being willing to ask hard questions, even when you'd rather not know the answers. If it *is* a phase, curiosity will do no harm. But if it is more than that, curiosity may be the very thing that interrupts the spiral before it deepens. When we lead with curiosity, we teach our loved one that their struggles are not shameful — they're signals. And signals, once noticed, can guide everyone toward help, healing, and hope.

Myth 2: "If I Bring It Up, I'll Make It Worse."

Few fears run deeper for parents than the fear of saying the wrong thing. When your loved one seems fragile, withdrawn, or on edge, every word can feel like a potential trigger. You worry that asking questions might make them defensive, that talking about substance use might "put ideas in their head," or that naming your concern might somehow invite rebellion. The instinct to stay quiet is understandable — it comes from love and the desire to protect. But silence, however well-intentioned, often sends the wrong message.

Silence can feel safe in the moment, but over time it breeds secrecy. Adolescents and young adults are exquisitely sensitive to tone, body language, and emotional energy. When a parent avoids a topic, they don't interpret it as neutrality — they often interpret it as discomfort, shame, or disapproval. The unspoken message becomes: *this is too uncomfortable to talk about.* For a young person who is already struggling with confusion, guilt, or fear, that silence can reinforce the belief that their pain is unacceptable.

Open, calm conversation is one of the most protective scaffoldings a parent can offer. Research consistently shows that early, nonjudgmental dialogue about stress, emotions, and coping reduces the risk of high-risk behaviors, including substance use. Communication does not cause the problem — it buffers against it. When parents initiate honest conversations, they normalize emotional expression, model curiosity, and signal that home/family is a safe place for truth. Think of openness as inoculation. Just as a vaccine introduces the body to a small, manageable exposure that builds immunity, honest communication helps the family develop emotional resilience before crises deepen. When parents talk openly about anxiety, sadness, or peer pressure, they equip their loved one with language and tools long before those challenges escalate. You're not planting ideas — you're planting safety.

Of course, these conversations are rarely comfortable. Many parents grew up in households where emotions were private and vulnerability was met with silence or discipline. Talking about mental health or substance use may feel unnatural or even taboo. The key is not to wait for the perfect words — it is to show up with the right tone. Calm, curious, and steady communication matters more than flawless phrasing. You don't need a script; you need sincerity.

You might begin with something simple, like:

"I've noticed you seem more tired lately. How have you been feeling?"

"There's been a lot of talk about stress and anxiety at school. How are you managing all that?"

"I read something about teens using substances to cope with pressure — is that something you've seen or felt tempted by?"

These are not interrogations; they're invitations. They communicate interest without intrusion. You're not demanding answers — you're making space for them. Even if your loved one shrugs, rolls their eyes, or changes the subject, the message still lands: *I'm here. I care. I can handle hard conversations.*

Parents often assume that talking about difficult topics will escalate the problem, but avoidance has the opposite effect. When no one talks about emotions or choices, shame fills the silence. Shame thrives in secrecy; it loses power in dialogue. When a loved one knows they can bring something home — whether it is a mistake, a fear, or a confession — without facing humiliation or panic, that trust becomes a lifeline. it is also important to remember that young people are already hearing about substances, stress, and mental health — from peers, social media, or the culture around them. The question isn't whether they'll be exposed to these ideas; it is who will help them make sense of the ideas. When parents remain silent, they surrender that influence to others. By speaking first, calmly and factually, you establish yourself as a safe source of truth.

The tone of these conversations matters more than the content. Most teens and young adults have a finely tuned radar for judgment. They can sense when questions are driven by fear rather than curiosity. The goal is to stay anchored in empathy — to listen more than you lecture, to reflect more than you react. If your loved one says something alarming, take a breath before responding.

"Thank you for telling me that. I'm glad you felt you could share it."

"That sounds like a lot to carry. Let's figure out what kind of support might help."

These responses communicate calm authority and emotional containment — you're not panicking, you're partnering.

For parents who fear that talking will somehow make things worse, it can help to reframe what "worse" really means. Temporary discomfort isn't danger. A defensive reaction isn't failure. Sometimes, difficult conversations feel tense precisely because they're hitting something true. The goal is not immediate resolution but sustained openness — to build a relational bridge strong enough to carry weight when it matters most.

When communication becomes a habit, it creates what family therapists call a "culture of approachability." This means that even when your loved one does not take you up on the offer to talk, they know it is available. Over time, that knowledge becomes a source of safety. When the moment comes — and it often does — when they're scared or ashamed or uncertain, they'll remember that you were willing to listen before they even knew what to say.

Bringing it up won't make it worse. Pretending it isn't there might. The courage to speak, even imperfectly, sends a message far louder than silence ever could: *You are not alone in this. I'm strong enough to face the truth with you.*

Openness is not about prying into every detail; it is about keeping the door unlocked. it is about letting your loved one know that, no matter what, there's space for honesty between you. That space — that steady, non-judgmental awareness — is what turns fear into connection and crisis into possibility.

Myth 3: "Tough Love Is the Only Way."

Few phrases have shaped the landscape of parenting and recovery culture more than *"tough love."* It has been passed down through generations as a kind of moral compass — the idea that true care means over control, that empathy equals enabling, and that the only way to motivate change is through consequence and withdrawal. Parents are told to "let them hit bottom," "stop rescuing," "show them the consequences." These messages often come from well-meaning friends, relatives, or even professionals, and while they contain kernels of truth, they can easily harden into rigidity.

The belief that firmness must equal harshness runs deep in our culture. it is rooted in the idea that suffering is the only teacher strong enough to provoke change. But what decades of research — and countless family stories — have shown is that punitive or emotionally distant approaches often backfire. They don't break denial; they tend to deepen shame. They don't inspire responsibility; they tend to breed resentment or despair. When young people feel rejected or unloved at the very moment that they most need connection, they don't learn accountability — they learn isolation.

This does not mean that boundaries are unimportant. On the contrary, clear limits are vital to safety and recovery. But boundaries and punishment are not the same thing. Boundaries communicate care; punishment communicates rejection. The difference lies in tone, intention, and follow-through. Saying, *"I can't allow you to come home high,"* is a limit — firm, clear, and rooted in safety. Saying, *"You're not welcome here until you get your act together,"* is exile. One holds the line while keeping the relationship intact; the other severs the connection and leaves the young person to navigate shame alone. The irony of "tough love" is that it often leaves both parent and loved one suffering. Parents who withdraw affection or cut off communication do so out of desperation, not cruelty. They're exhausted, frightened, and often following advice that tells them love is dangerous — that empathy will "feed the problem." Yet when parents act from fear rather than grounded conviction, they feel hollow afterward. They miss their loved one. They wonder if they went too far. They lie awake replaying the last conversation, unsure whether the silence they imposed is protecting or harming.

What families need instead is what we might call *steady love.* Steady love is not permissive or naive. It does not mean tolerating harmful behavior or pretending everything is fine. It means remaining emotionally anchored even as you set limits. it is the capacity to say, *"I love you too much to support choices that hurt you — and I will not stop loving you because you're struggling."* That balance — of clarity and compassion, of boundary and belonging — is what helps families survive the chaos of substance use and mental health crises.

In clinical work, this approach is sometimes referred to as "authoritative warmth" — the style of parenting most strongly linked to resilience. It combines firm expectations with emotional responsiveness. The parent stays in the role of guide, not adversary. They use limits to create safety, not shame. They model accountability while maintaining empathy. Instead of *"You're on your own,"* the message becomes *"We're in this together, but I can't make your choices for you."* That distinction preserves dignity — for both parent and loved one.

It is also important to understand that connection does not mean rescuing. Steady love still honors natural consequences. it is not about preventing discomfort; it is about ensuring that discomfort leads to learning, not despair. For example, a parent might say, *"If you choose not to follow treatment recommendations, I can't provide financial support right now — but I'm still here to talk, and I'll always help you find help."* The consequence remains, but it is delivered with compassion, not condemnation. The door to relationship stays open. Families that practice steady love often describe a subtle shift: conversations become less reactive and more honest. The loved one may still test boundaries, but they no longer feel abandoned when those boundaries appear. Over time, this creates what therapists call *relational safety* — the sense that love isn't contingent on perfection. That safety is largely what makes self-reflection possible. A young person who feels seen and loved even in their mistakes is far more likely to accept help than one who feels punished or exiled.

Tough love without connection does not heal; it isolates. It tells the struggling person, *You are lovable only when you are well.* But steady love says, *You are lovable, period — and because of that, I will stay consistent even when things get hard.* That consistency is likely to become the ground beneath a family's feet. It keeps communication open when everything else feels uncertain.

Parents often worry that compassion will weaken their authority. In truth, compassion tends to give authority meaning. Rules without relationship breed rebellion. Boundaries delivered with empathy invite accountability. When love remains steady, limits begin to feel less like control and more like care. "Tough love" is a seductive phrase because it promises simplicity — a clear formula in a world that feels chaotic. But families are not formulas; they're ecosystems. And ecosystems thrive on balance: warmth and firmness, truth and tenderness, boundary and belonging. The real work of parenting through substance use and recovery is not to become harder, but steadier — to learn how to stand firm without closing your heart.

Ultimately, love isn't what enables dysfunction; love is what makes healing possible.

Myth 4: "If We Were Better Parents, This Wouldn't Happen."

Few myths cut deeper than the one that blames the family. When a loved one struggles with substance use or mental health challenges, parents often turn inward before they turn outward. They replay decisions in their minds — the schools they chose, the rules they set, the moments they lost their temper or looked away. They measure themselves against other families who seem to have it all together and quietly wonder, *what did we miss? What did we do wrong?*

This myth survives because it offers an illusion of control. If the problem is your fault, then theoretically, you could have prevented it — or could fix it now. Blame, even self-blame, feels safer than helplessness. Reality is far more complex. Addiction and mental health disorders inherently cross every demographic, every neighborhood, every family system. They don't discriminate by income, parenting style, or moral compass. They are biopsychosocial conditions — influenced by genetics, brain chemistry, trauma history, social context, and timing. Good parenting cannot guarantee immunity from suffering, just as good health habits cannot eliminate every illness.

Yet guilt is powerful. It sneaks into even the most well-intentioned thoughts: *If I had been stricter... if I had been softer... if I hadn't worked so much... if I had paid more attention.* "If onlys" can become endless. Parents begin to carry invisible weight, moving through each day with the quiet ache of regret. They may overcompensate, trying to control or fix what feels broken. Or they may withdraw, convinced they have lost the right to lead. Either way, guilt shifts energy inward — away from connection and toward self-punishment.

Guilt, while understandable, is not the same as responsibility. Guilt asks, *who caused this?* Responsibility asks, *what can we do now?* The first keeps you trapped in the past; the second points you toward healing.

It is also worth noting that guilt often hides love. Parents who blame themselves do so because they care deeply. They too often would rather shoulder pain themselves than believe their loved one is suffering beyond their reach. In that sense, guilt is an act of devotion — but one that needs to evolve. When guilt lingers too long, it becomes paralysis. It keeps families stuck in shame instead of moving toward change. From a clinical perspective, shame-based thinking often interferes with a parent's ability to be effective. When you believe you have failed, it is harder to set boundaries, to stay calm, or to trust your own instincts. Shame makes you reactive. It leads to overcorrection — either becoming overly permissive to "make up for mistakes" or overly punitive to "regain control." Both extremes miss the middle ground of compassionate leadership that teens and young adults most need. The truth is, parenting a loved one through substance use or mental health issues is not a test of worth; it is a call to growth. Every family system will be challenged by something — loss, illness, identity, change. This happens to be the challenge your family is facing. It does not define your goodness or your love. What defines you now is how you respond.

Healing begins when the family shifts from blame to understanding — from "Why did this happen to us?" to "What are we learning through this?" This reframe allows parents to see themselves not as failures, but as participants in recovery. Instead of carrying guilt as a burden, they begin to use awareness as a resource. They learn new ways to communicate, to regulate, to connect. They stop trying to undo the past and start showing up fully in the present.

it is also important to remember that adolescents and young adults don't need perfect parents — they need attuned ones. They need adults who can model self-reflection, repair, and resilience. When you can say to your loved one, *I wish I had seen things sooner, but I'm here now and ready to listen,* you teach them something profound: that accountability is not the same as shame, and that love can withstand imperfection.

Families that recover together often describe a paradox — that healing came not from fixing everything, but from telling the truth about what was hard. They began to see that the moments of disconnection were not evidence of failure; they were invitations to repair. In that sense, the crisis itself can become a teacher. It reveals old patterns that need updating, boundaries that need redefining, and ways of relating that need more empathy. No parent can rewrite the past, but every parent can rewrite the story that begins now. The question is never *"What did we do wrong?"* The real question — the one that leads forward — is *"What can we do now that we know?"* That question opens space for possibility. It replaces guilt with agency. It allows you to act, learn, and grow alongside your loved one rather than against them.

When you shift from blame to presence, something remarkable happens: your loved one begins to feel safer. They sense that the focus is no longer on fault but on healing. They see a parent who is steady enough to look reality in the eye and compassionate enough to keep reaching out. That combination — humility and love — is what rebuilds trust after pain. If you find yourself tangled in guilt, remember this: You are not the cause of your loved one's struggle, but you are an essential part of their recovery. Your love still matters. Your presence still counts. Healing is not about erasing what came before; it is about transforming it into wisdom, empathy, and connection.

The myth of the "better parent" tends to divide — it pits you against yourself. But the truth of healing unites — it invites you back into a relationship, with your loved one and with your own humanity. You don't need to be better. You only need to be here, willing, and real. That's where every story of recovery begins.

Myth 5: "They Have to Hit Rock Bottom Before They'll Change."

Of all the phrases that circulate in conversations about addiction, few are as well-known — or as harmful — as *"They have to hit rock bottom before they'll change."* it is repeated so often that it sounds like wisdom, a hard truth learned through experience. But while it may once have reflected a particular moment in addiction recovery culture, today it is dangerously outdated. Rock bottom is not a therapeutic intervention; it is a crisis point. And waiting for someone you love to collapse before seeking help risks consequences that can't always be undone. The idea of "rock bottom" grew out of early recovery models that viewed suffering as the necessary catalyst for change. The belief was that people had to lose everything — health, relationships, stability — before they could become "ready." But decades of research in neuroscience, trauma, and behavior change have shown a more accurate picture: readiness is not a single moment; it is a process, and it grows in the presence of safety, not despair. The human brain does not learn best under threat — it learns in environments where it feels seen, supported, and guided.

If we equate transformation with suffering, we are likely to confuse collapse with insight. Rock bottom isn't an awakening; it is the point where pain outweighs resources. It can indeed become a turning point, but it is a dangerous one to wait for — especially in adolescence and young adulthood, when the line between crisis and catastrophe is heartbreakingly thin. The risks of overdose, self-harm, trauma, or long-term psychological damage increase when help comes too late. There's nothing noble about letting someone spiral into danger to "teach them a lesson." Change becomes possible not through suffering, but through connection and structure. Young people rarely heal because they have been broken; they heal because they have been held up. Early, compassionate intervention — grounded in consistency, boundaries, and genuine empathy — can interrupt destructive cycles long before they reach crisis. That's not enabling; that's prevention.

The myth of rock bottom also places an unbearable burden on parents. It tells them to step aside, to detach, to watch from a distance while their loved one suffers. For many, that feels like emotional torture. Parents describe lying awake at night, torn between professional advice that says, *"Don't rescue them,"* and an instinct that screams, *"But what if they don't survive this?"* This conflict — between clinical detachment and parental love — leaves families frozen in fear. But the truth is, love and boundaries can coexist. You don't have to choose between caring and protecting yourself.

Early support does not mean doing the work *for* your loved one. It means creating conditions where change becomes possible. It means recognizing that shame shuts down growth, while belonging reawakens it. You can say, *"I can't support your choices, but I'll always support your healing."* That's not rescuing; that's relational accountability. it is the steady, compassionate stance that allows a young person to begin imagining a life beyond crisis.

Clinically, we know that readiness for change is dynamic. It ebbs and flows — sometimes within the same day. The right kind of intervention at the right time can shift that readiness dramatically. A conversation that communicates care rather than condemnation, a therapist who validates without excusing, a family who sets clear but loving limits are the factors that move someone toward recovery long before they hit an imagined "bottom." it is also worth noting that "bottom" looks different for everyone. For one person, it might be an academic suspension; for another, a relationship ending; for another, an overdose or hospitalization. There is no universal threshold of suffering that guarantees change. Some people never reach that point at all — they die before they get the chance.

When parents learn to intervene early — with compassion, structure, and calm persistence — they model a different version of strength. They show their teen or young adult that love does not mean rescuing, but it also does not mean abandoning. They embody the paradox at the heart of recovery: that connection and accountability are not opposites, but partners. A parent can say, *"We can't ignore what's happening, and we also don't have to wait for disaster."* Early intervention also challenges the shame that keeps families silent. Too often, parents wait because they fear judgment — from friends, from schools, from the community. They tell themselves, *"Maybe it is not that bad yet."* But help-seeking isn't a declaration of failure; it is an act of leadership. The earlier a family brings a concern into the light, the greater the chance of recovery without crisis.

Another layer to this myth deserves attention: it often arises from exhaustion. When parents have tried everything — the talks, the rules, the pleas — they begin to lose hope. "Rock bottom" becomes a coping mechanism, a way to explain what feels unfixable. It offers distance from pain: *Maybe if I stop trying, something will finally change.* That exhaustion is real and deeply human. But the path forward is not withdrawal — it is recalibration. It is finding new ways to engage that are sustainable, provide boundaries, and emotionally honest.

Rock bottom is not a prerequisite for growth. It is a warning sign of systems that waited too long. The more we understand addiction and emotional distress as chronic, treatable conditions rather than moral failings, the more we can see that waiting for collapse is not compassionate — it is too often dangerous.

Families don't need to be perfect; they need to be proactive. Compassionate, informed engagement — early and often — saves lives. Rock bottom isn't inevitable. it is preventable. And every time a parent reaches out before the crisis, every time a family replaces judgment with curiosity and fear with steadiness, the bottom gets a little higher, the landing a little softer, and the chance for recovery that much stronger.

The Role of Shame

Myths thrive in the soil of shame. Shame is the quiet undertow beneath so many family struggles — the invisible force that convinces parents to hide, to isolate, to behave normally even when everything inside the home feels like it is falling apart. It is the voice that says, *If people knew, they'd judge us. If we ask for help, it means we failed.* Shame narrows a family's world. It draws curtains, lowers voices, and builds walls where bridges are needed most.

Shame is not just an emotion; it is a social survival instinct. It evolved to help us stay connected to the group by alerting us to threats of rejection. But in the context of mental health and substance use, shame becomes distorted. It tells families that struggle equals deficiency — that a functional family wouldn't have these problems, that good parents would have seen it sooner, stopped it sooner, fixed it sooner. These are falsehoods that shame tells to keep pain hidden, but hidden pain only deepens. Many parents live a kind of double life during these times. On the outside, they keep up appearances — attend school events, go to work, exchange polite smiles with neighbors. Inside, they are terrified. They check their phones at night, waiting for messages that may not come. They rehearse excuses for missed assignments, canceled plans, or withdrawn behavior. Every interaction becomes a quiet performance designed to protect the family's image. Yet, this secrecy isolates. It turns suffering into something that feels private, even when it is profoundly human.

Clinically, shame functions like emotional quicksand. The more families struggle against it, the deeper it tends to pull. It feeds myths like "this is our fault," "we shouldn't talk about it," or "if we just try harder, it will go away." Shame invariably thrives in silence; it cannot survive exposure. But breaking that silence can feel terrifying. Parents worry that sharing their truth will lead to judgment or pity — that they'll be defined by their loved one's behavior rather than by their love. What they rarely realize is that their silence often reinforces the very stigma they fear.

Breaking free from shame begins with one small act of courage: telling the truth, even to a trusted person. It does not have to be public or dramatic. It might be a quiet confession to a close friend, a conversation with a therapist, or a moment of honesty in a support group. Saying, *"we're struggling, and I don't know what to do,"* is not weakness — it is the first act of healing. It is how light begins to enter the places shame has kept dark. Families who share their struggles often discover something remarkable: they are not alone. The illusion of isolation begins to crack. Behind virtually every confident parent at a school event, every seemingly intact family, there are stories of fear, worry, and loss. When one person speaks honestly, others exhale. Someone says, *"us too."* Connection begins. And connection is what dissolves stigma.

Shame tells families they are different; connection from truth and honestly reminds them they are human. The simple act of being heard — of having someone meet your pain with empathy instead of judgment — can recalibrate the entire emotional system. It serves to restore dignity. It serves to transform private suffering into shared humanity. Research on trauma and resilience suggests that what heals people most deeply is not the absence of struggle but the presence of understanding. When shame loses its secrecy, myths begin to lose their power. The stories that once kept families trapped — *it is our fault, they have to hit bottom, tough love is the only way* — begin to unravel under the light of truth. Parents realize that these myths were never moral truths, only coping mechanisms shaped by fear. And when fear no longer runs the story, love and reason can return to the table.

This process does not happen all at once. The first time a parent speaks honestly about their loved one's substance use or mental health crisis, their voice may shake. They may feel exposed. But vulnerability should not be mistaken for fragility — it is strength in motion. Each time the truth is spoken, shame's grip weakens. Each time a family reaches out — to a therapist, a group, a friend — they expand their circle of safety. With that expansion comes a sense of breath, of possibility.

In family therapy, we often describe this shift as moving from secrecy to story. Secrecy hides; story integrates. Secrecy says, *this shouldn't have happened.* Story says, *this is part of our history, and we're learning from it.* When a family begins to tell its story, healing begins — not because the past changes, but because meaning emerges. For parents, this reframe is powerful. It allows them to see themselves not as broken, but as brave. It helps them understand that the most helpful thing they can do for their loved one — and for themselves — is to live truthfully. There is no shame in struggle; there is only shame in silence, and even that can be unlearned.

The role of shame in keeping myths alive cannot be overstated, but neither can the power of honesty in dismantling them. Every time a parent chooses connection over concealment, every time a family tells the truth rather than performing perfection, the culture around them begins to shift. Other families see that openness is possible, that healing does not require hiding, and that love can exist alongside imperfection.

Shame isolates, but truth invites company. The moment we speak — even quietly, even trembling — we begin to find one another. And in that shared space, myths lose their grip, families regain their voice, and the long work of healing begins to feel not only possible, but shared.

Replacing Myths with Truths

Myth	Reality
"This is just a phase."	Early intervention prevents escalation. Patterns matter more than isolated behaviors.
"If I talk about it, I'll make it worse."	Honest, calm dialogue reduces secrecy and shame.
"Tough love is the only way."	Compassionate boundaries protect without alienating.
"We caused this."	Focus on contributions to healing, not causation.

"They must hit rock bottom."

Recovery can begin at any stage — safety first.

Reflection & Awareness

1. **Name one belief** you have held that might have kept you from seeking help sooner. Where did it come from — culture, family, fear?
2. **Rewrite that belief** into a statement that supports action instead of avoidance. Example: "I can talk about this without shame."
3. **Share your story** with one safe person or community. Saying the words aloud begins to break the myth's hold.
4. **Remember:** awareness is an act of courage, not failure. Myths lose their power the moment we speak truth aloud.

Myths usually begin as protection — a way to make sense of what feels unbearable. But protection becomes a prison when it stops us from reaching for help. When we replace myth with understanding, fear gives way to possibility. Families begin to move, however slowly, toward healing grounded not in illusion, but in truth.

Chapter 3

Communication That Connects, Not Controls

> **When we listen with the intent to understand rather than to fix, we create the conditions for change**

Virtually every parent of a struggling adolescent or young adult eventually reaches a moment when words seem to lose their meaning. You ask how school went and hear, "Fine." You ask again and get a shrug. You try a different tone, and a door slams. The loved one who once narrated every detail of their day now lives behind silence or sarcasm. What used to be easy — a shared meal, a quick check-in — begins to feel like navigating a minefield. When mental health challenges or substance use enter the picture, that silence can feel unbearable. Parents feel the distance growing and instinctively try to bridge it. They lean in harder — more questions, more reminders, more reasoning. They explain, plead, or warn, hoping that logic will pull their loved one back to safety. But what love intends as concern, a young person's nervous system often hears as pressure. The more parents reach for words, the more those words seem to ricochet off invisible walls.

To understand why, it helps to remember that during adolescence and young adulthood, the brain is still under construction. The areas responsible for emotional regulation and decision-making keep developing, while the limbic system — the emotional center — is on overdrive. This means that teens and young adults often interpret tone, volume, and facial expression before they even register content. A well-intentioned, "I'm worried about you," might sound like an accusation. A calm question might feel like an interrogation.

Urgency and love can sound identical to a parent — but to a loved one in distress, urgency often lands as threat. When a parent's voice tightens, their loved one's body reacts, not to the words, but to the energy behind them. The nervous system, sensing potential conflict, shifts into defense mode. What follows is the familiar pattern: the parent escalates out of fear; the loved one tends to withdraw out of self-protection. Each side believes they are reacting to the other's behavior, but in truth, both are reacting to fear. The painful paradox is that silence often grows strongest where love is deepest. Parents push hardest when they're scared because they care deeply. Teens and young adults retreat because they're overwhelmed, not indifferent. Both are trying to protect the relationship in their own way — the parent by reaching out, the loved one by pulling away. The result is a stalemate: two nervous systems circling one another, each longing to connect but unsure how.

If communication is the lifeline between parent and their loved one, the early stages of crisis are when the rope begins to fray. The parent may tug harder, hoping to pull their loved one back; the loved one may pull away, needing space to breathe. The tension stretches until something breaks — the conversation, the trust, or the parent's sense of confidence. Many parents describe feeling like they have "lost their kid" long before treatment ever begins. The house is full, but the connection feels empty. It is important to recognize that when words stop working, it is not a sign of failure. It is a sign of overload. The system — both parent and loved one — is operating at emotional capacity. In that state, words alone can't repair what nervous systems are still fighting to survive. Communication has to shift from persuasion to presence, from explanation to empathy. The goal is not to say the perfect thing; it is to create enough safety for words to start mattering again.

Repairing that lifeline begins with understanding the difference between talking *to* and connecting *with.* Talking *to* focuses on content — grades, choices, curfews, consequences. Connecting *with* focuses on context — emotion, experience, meaning. When parents prioritize *with* over *to,* the nervous system begins to settle. The loved one no longer feels cornered; they feel seen. That does not mean abandoning structure or pretending everything is fine. It means remembering that how you speak is often more important than what you say. A calm, grounded tone communicates safety. A slower pace signals presence. Even brief, consistent gestures of curiosity — "You seem quiet today," or "Rough day?" — are small acts of repair. When these gestures are genuine and without a hidden agenda, they remind your loved one that communication is still possible, even in tension.

Parents sometimes ask, "But what if they don't want to talk at all?" The answer is: you can still communicate safety without words. Communication happens in energy, in consistency, in what your presence conveys. When you stay calm in the face of anger, or maintain respect even when boundaries are tested, you're saying something profound: *This relationship can hold hard things.*

The good news is that language can heal, but not in the way most parents imagine. Healing communication does not come from perfect phrasing — it comes from regulated nervous systems. When a parent can manage their own fear, the loved one's body senses it, even before they hear the words. Calmness invites curiosity. Curiosity invites dialogue. And dialogue, over time, rebuilds trust.

This chapter is about repairing that rope — strand by strand — with curiosity, empathy, and structure. Curiosity allows you to see beyond the behavior to the emotion beneath. Empathy softens the defensive walls that both you and your loved one have built to survive. Structure ensures that love remains consistent even when circumstances are chaotic. Together, they form a kind of emotional scaffolding — a framework strong enough to support growth, but flexible enough to bend with the storm. Parents often expect communication repair to happen through one big conversation — a heart-to-heart that changes everything. In reality, it happens through dozens of small ones. It happens in the way you greet them in the morning, how you respond when they test limits, how you manage your own tone when you're scared. Each interaction is a strand of that rope. Some days, you may only add one thread. Other days, you might mend a whole section. What matters is that you keep showing up to the work — not because you always know what to say, but because you refuse to let silence have the final word.

When words stop working, what begins to heal communication usually isn't eloquence — it is presence. The quiet strength of a parent who can say, *"I don't have all the answers, but I'm here, and I'm listening,"* speaks louder than any lecture ever could. That steadiness becomes the signal through the noise — a reminder, to both parent and loved one, that even when language falters, love can still be heard.

Why Communication Breaks Down

Parents often describe talking to their adolescent or young adult as "walking on eggshells." Conversations that start with good intentions can quickly derail — what begins as a question turns into an argument, what was meant as concern is heard as criticism. The harder parents try to reason, the faster the situation escalates. It can feel like speaking two different languages. In a way, it is.

To understand why communication breaks down so easily during adolescence and young adulthood, it helps to look at what's happening inside the brain. During these years, the emotional center — the amygdala and broader limbic system — develops long before the reasoning center, the prefrontal cortex. The amygdala is responsible for detecting threat and generating strong emotional responses like fear, anger, or excitement. The prefrontal cortex, by contrast, manages impulse control, long-term planning, and empathy. In other words, the part of the brain that feels is fully online years before the part that regulates. This developmental gap explains much of the volatility parents see: fast feelings, slow logic. When your teen slams the door after a minor disagreement or bursts into tears over a seemingly small disappointment, it is not manipulation — it is neurobiology. Their emotional system is running at full speed, while their ability to self-regulate is still catching up. Add the disinhibiting effects of substances, trauma, or untreated mental health symptoms — like anxiety, depression, or ADHD — and the result is a nervous system that fluctuates between overdrive and shutdown. You see it as explosive anger, withdrawal, avoidance, or defensiveness. They experience it as overwhelming.

When communication breaks down, most parents instinctively lean harder into explanation. They try to reason their way toward calm: *"If you would just listen..." "You know better than this..." "Here's why that does not make sense..."* But reasoning with someone whose nervous system is flooded rarely works — not because they don't care, but because in that state they can't process what you're saying. The still developing prefrontal cortex, the part of the brain that handles logic and empathy, goes offline when the body senses threat.

What many parents don't realize is that *intensity feels like a threat* to an already dysregulated brain. When you raise your voice, use strong language, or over-explain, you're speaking to the wrong part of your loved one's brain. You're trying to communicate with the operator when the alarm is blaring. And when the alarm is sounding, the only thing the brain can focus on is survival — fight, flight, freeze, or fawn. This does not mean you can never express emotion. It means that timing and tone are everything. Meeting intensity with intensity only reinforces the sense of danger. A parent's frustration, even when justified, can sound like rejection to a young person whose internal alarm system is already hypersensitive. The louder you get, the less they hear. The more you explain, the more they feel misunderstood. It is not defiance; it is neurophysiology.

When parents understand this, something important shifts. They stop taking the behavior so personally. They realize that their loved one's reaction — whether explosive or withdrawn — isn't a verdict on their parenting but a reflection of an overloaded system. That recognition allows compassion to enter the room, and compassion is what begins to repair connection. Safety — not logic — is what opens the door. When your teen or young adult feels emotionally safe, the brain's immature prefrontal cortex re-engages, allowing reflection, empathy, and problem-solving to return. Safety does not mean agreeing with everything they say or letting go of boundaries. It means creating an emotional environment where the body does not feel under attack. That environment is built through tone, pacing, facial expression, and nonverbal cues as much as through words.

In family therapy, we often say, *regulate before you communicate.* If you're elevated — angry, anxious, or desperate — your nervous system is speaking even louder than your voice. The first task is to steady yourself. Take a breath. Lower your tone. Slow your speech. These small physiological shifts signal to your loved one's nervous system, *We're safe. I'm not your enemy.* Once the threat response subsides, real communication can begin.

You might notice that the best conversations with your loved one happen when neither of you is trying too hard — in the car, on a walk, while cooking together. These are moments when pressure is low and presence is high. There's no eye contact demanding performance, no intensity demanding answers. Safety allows authenticity to emerge. It is not magic; it is biology. The nervous system opens when it does not feel trapped. For parents, this realization can be both humbling and freeing. It means that your words matter less than your presence. It also means that you don't have to have the perfect response every time. Your calmness is the intervention. When your loved one storms off and you don't follow with anger, you're showing them something their own brain can't yet do: stay steady in the storm. Over time, they begin to internalize that model of regulation. Your calm becomes their roadmap.

It is also important to note that safety is not per-missiveness. Setting boundaries is still essential — it is that boundaries delivered in safety land differently from boundaries delivered in fear. Saying, *"I'm not okay with you coming home intoxicated. We'll talk about it in the morning,"* communicates firmness and containment without humil-iation. The message becomes: *I love you, and I won't let this behavior harm you or us.* That blend of care and clarity is what builds long-term trust. When parents begin to see communication through the lens of the nervous system rather than morality, the entire dynamic changes. Instead of labeling your teen as "ungrateful," "lazy," or "manipu-lative," you start to see them as dysregulated, scared, or struggling. That shift does not excuse harmful behavior — it contextualizes it. And context is what makes compas-sion possible.

In the end, communication between parents and their adolescent or young adult children isn't about winning ar-guments or getting quick answers. It is about staying con-nected through uncertainty. When words stop working, regulation becomes the bridge. When logic fails, safety restores the signal. Every moment of calm presence — every time you respond rather than react — strengthens the rope that connects you and your loved one.

And that rope, even when frayed, is not beyond repair.

The Shift from Control to Connection

Most parents enter difficult conversations with the best of intentions. They want to help their loved one understand the consequences of their choices, make better decisions, and avoid danger. But under stress — especially when fear and love collide — those intentions often translate into correction rather than connection. The instinct to *teach* takes over. Parents explain, remind, and reason, believing that if they can just say the right words, their loved one will finally "get it." But recovery and growth don't work that way. You cannot argue a teen or young adult into insight. Insight is not forced; it is invited. It happens when a young person feels emotionally safe enough to reflect on their own experience without being shamed or cornered. That's why, in recovery work, the goal of communication isn't correction — it is connection. Connection does not mean approval or agreement; it means creating the relational conditions in which learning and accountability can take root.

The stance of control sounds like: *"You need to explain why you did this."* It demands justification. It starts from a position of authority and assumes that logic will lead to change. But when someone is dysregulated, frightened, or ashamed, logic feels like interrogation. The nervous system closes, and the mind stops listening. The stance of connection, on the other hand, sounds like: *"I want to understand what this is like for you."* It is a posture of curiosity rather than judgment. It signals that you are not here to win, but to witness. That single shift — from *explain yourself* to *help me understand* — changes everything. It tells your loved one's nervous system: *You're not in trouble right now. You're safe enough to tell the truth.* And only in that safety can reflection begin.

Parents might worry that connection before correction is permissive — that it sends the wrong message, that it lets the behavior slide. But connection first, correction second isn't permissive; it is strategic. Regulation always precedes reflection. When a young person feels emotionally flooded, they can't absorb feedback or make rational decisions. Their body is busy managing threat, not processing meaning. The moment you create safety — through tone, patience, or simple presence — the prefrontal cortex (the reasoning part of the brain) begins to re-engage. Only then does your loved one have access to insight.

Think of it like CPR for communication: you have to restore breath before you can restore words. When the nervous system calms, the mind reopens. That's when lessons, boundaries, and consequences actually land.

This shift — from control to connection — is both subtle and profound. It asks parents to move from being the *enforcer of right behavior* to the *facilitator of self-awareness.* It means trading power struggles for partnership, replacing lectures with listening, and redefining what it means to lead. Leadership in this context is not about dominance; it is about containment — holding steady enough for both of you to come back into regulation. When a parent says, *"You need to explain why you did this,"* the underlying message is, *you owe me an answer to make my fear go away.* When a parent says, *"Help me understand what this feels like for you,"* the message becomes, *you matter more than the mistake you made.* One approach seeks control; the other builds trust.

The truth is that most adolescents and young adults already know when they have crossed a line. What they often lack is not awareness of their actions, but the capacity to face them without shame. When a parent meets them with curiosity instead of condemnation, that shame begins to soften. And when shame softens, accountability becomes possible.

This does not mean abandoning consequences or boundaries. It means sequencing them correctly. Connection first ensures that any boundary you set will be heard, not resisted. Correction offered before connection feels like punishment; correction offered after connection feels like guidance. The words might be the same, but the delivery — and therefore the impact — is entirely different.

For example:

Control stance: *"You broke our trust again. You're grounded until you learn your lesson."*

Connection stance: *"I can see how much you're struggling right now, and we still need to talk about what happens next. I want to understand what made this feel worth the risk."*

Both acknowledge the problem, but only one invites dialogue. The second creates space for learning — for both of you. It models emotional regulation and respect, even in conflict. Over time, this pattern teaches your loved one how to self-regulate, because they are experiencing regulation in real time through you.

Connection is not about letting go of authority; it is about using your authority wisely. Adolescents and young adults need to know that their parents can hold boundaries *and* their emotions at the same time. When you stay calm, you're not just managing behavior — you're shaping the internal voice your loved one will one day use to manage their own. You're teaching them what accountability sounds like when it is paired with love. It takes immense discipline to pause in moments of fear and choose connection over control. Every fiber of your protective instinct will want to fix, explain, or demand answers. But real authority — the kind that earns trust rather than fear — comes from restraint, not reaction. The quieter you become, the more your presence speaks.

This shift also transforms the atmosphere in the home. Conversations that once felt like battles become opportunities for understanding. You begin to see that connection does not undermine boundaries — it strengthens them. When a young person feels seen, they're more likely to comply, not because they have been coerced, but because they feel respected. Respect is reciprocal. It grows in the space that control once occupied.

Ultimately, the transition from control to connection mirrors the very process of recovery itself. It is about surrender — not in the sense of giving up, but of letting go of the illusion that you can force change. You can't make someone heal. You can only make it safe enough for healing to begin. When you adopt the stance of connection — *I want to understand what this is like for you* — you are speaking to the part of your loved one that still hopes, still wants to belong, still wants to be seen. You are sending the message: *You are worth knowing, even now.*

And that, more than any lecture or punishment, is what opens the door to change.

Listening beneath the Surface

One of the most profound shifts parents can make in communication is learning to listen for what's *beneath* the words rather than reacting to what's on the surface. At times, teens and young adults don't speak their primary emotion. Instead, they communicate in code — a language shaped by vulnerability, pride, and fear. "I don't care" often means "I'm scared." "Leave me alone" can mean "I don't want to disappoint you." Even "You don't understand me" may translate to "I wish you could."

To the untrained ear, these statements sound dismissive or defiant. But beneath them are layers of unspoken meaning — often confusion, shame, or longing. Adolescents and young adults are in the midst of defining who they are and where they belong. That developmental task is tender and uncertain. When life feels too big, they protect themselves through tone and attitude. Sarcasm, withdrawal, and defensiveness aren't evidence of apathy; they're signals of overwhelm. Listening beneath the surface means tuning in to affect, not just content. Affect is the emotional energy underneath the words — the tone, the facial expression, the pace of speech, the shift in posture. It is the part of communication that's felt more than heard. When you listen this way, you begin to hear emotion instead of opposition. You stop getting caught in the exact words and start responding to the feeling that's trying to be expressed.

For example, when your loved one rolls their eyes and mutters, "You're overreacting," the surface message sounds like dismissal. The instinctive response might be to defend yourself: *"I'm not overreacting! You're the one who—"* And just like that, the conversation becomes a battle of perspectives. But if you listen beneath the surface, you'll hear something else: *"I feel criticized,"* or *"I'm tired of disappointing you,"* or *"I need space."* When you respond to that underlying emotion instead of the literal words, everything shifts. You might say, *"It sounds like you feel I'm on your case all the time. That must be exhausting."* This isn't agreement — it is acknowledgment. You're not saying they're right; you're saying you're listening. Acknowledgment is the bridge between defensiveness and dialogue. Once someone feels understood, they no longer need to fight to prove their perspective. The nervous system relaxes. The wall is lowered and conversation becomes possible again.

In therapy, this process is called reflective listening or attunement — the act of mirroring not the content but the emotion of another person's communication. Attunement does not require you to fix or solve anything; it simply requires presence. It says, *"I see you trying to express something, even if it is coming out sideways."* That small recognition can diffuse tension faster than any logical argument ever could.

Listening beneath the surface also means resisting the urge to interpret too quickly. Many parents, especially those accustomed to solving problems, move straight to analysis: *"You're saying that because you're anxious,"* or *"You're just being defensive."* Even if accurate, these statements feel intrusive. They tell your loved one how they feel instead of showing that you're willing to feel *with* them. it is often more effective to reflect what you observe gently: *"You sound frustrated,"* or *"This seems really hard to talk about."* This keeps the door open for correction or elaboration — and it preserves your loved one's dignity in the process.

When parents master this kind of listening, something remarkable happens: the emotional temperature in the household begins to drop. Conversations that used to spiral into shouting or silence begin to unfold more softly. You start to see that most conflicts aren't about rules, curfews, or phone use — they're about belonging, autonomy, and trust. The argument about grades might really be about fear of failure. The argument about friends might really be about wanting to fit in. The argument about boundaries might really be about wanting to feel competent and independent.

It is natural to want to correct misinformation or defend your perspective, especially when the stakes feel high. But correction without connection always backfires. If your loved one does not feel heard, they'll keep repeating themselves — louder, harsher, more dramatically — until they do. When you validate the emotion first, you satisfy the nervous system's primary need: to feel seen and safe. Once that need is met, logic and reasoning can return to the table.

Parents sometimes worry that empathy sounds like endorsement. It does not. Saying, *"It sounds like you're really angry that I took the car keys,"* is not the same as saying, *"You were right to take the car without permission."* Empathy and agreement are not synonyms. Empathy is acknowledgment without surrender. It is a statement of connection, not compliance.

Listening beneath the surface also requires patience with silence. Teens and young adults often communicate through withdrawal — one-word answers, long pauses, distracted gestures. Parents can mistake these as rejection, but silence is often a sign of emotional processing. When you allow quiet without rushing to fill it, you communicate trust. You say, *"I can handle this pace. I don't need to push you."* That calm containment is especially healing for young people who feel chronically misunderstood. The practice of listening beneath the surface takes time to learn because it requires parents to manage their own internal reactions. When your loved one's words sting — *"You don't get it," "You make everything worse," "I hate this family"* — the instinct is to defend or withdraw. But those moments are when listening matters most. Underneath even the harshest words, there is often fear, grief, or longing for connection. If you can stay steady and hear the need beneath the noise, you model a kind of resilience your loved one can eventually internalize.

You don't have to get it perfectly. Even small moments of accurate empathy make a difference. A simple, *"That must be hard,"* or *"I can tell you don't want to talk right now, but I'm here when you're ready,"* communicates safety. Over time, these micro-moments of understanding rebuild the bridge between you.

Listening beneath the surface is not a communication tactic — it is a posture of love. It is the willingness to hear not only the words your loved one speaks but the emotions they can't yet name. It is the practice of remembering that beneath anger there is usually fear, and beneath distance there is often longing. When you listen this way, you become not just a parent trying to get through to their loved one, but a partner in their healing.

And that, ultimately, is what transforms communication from survival to connection: the steady choice to hear what is *felt,* not just what is *said.*

Validation: The Language of Safety

Validation is one of the most powerful — and often most misunderstood — tools a parent can use. To validate someone is to say, *"Your feelings make sense given what you've been through."* It is not the same as agreeing with their choices or condoning harmful behavior. Validation acknowledges experience, it doesn't endorse behavior. It communicates that you see the internal logic behind the feeling, even if you can't support the action that followed.

For many parents, this distinction feels tricky at first. They worry that if they validate their teen's or young adult's emotions, they'll be giving permission — that saying *"It makes sense you'd want to escape when everything feels overwhelming"* somehow encourages escape. But the opposite is true. Validation does not fuel unhealthy behavior; it disarms the shame that keeps that behavior alive. It tells your loved one, *"You're not bad for feeling this way. You're human."* And when someone feels seen and validated, they can begin to take responsibility rather than hide in guilt or defensiveness.

When you say, *"It makes sense you'd want to escape when everything feels overwhelming,"* you're not endorsing avoidance — you're naming the emotional logic behind it. You're recognizing that the desire to numb or withdraw often arises from pain too big to hold. You're saying, *"I get that this is hard."* That acknowledgment lowers the walls of self-protection and allows curiosity to enter the room: *"If this makes sense, then maybe there's another way to cope."* Likewise, when you say, *"I can see that you're angry and tired of people telling you what to do,"* you're not saying defiance is acceptable. You're saying, *"I understand how trapped you feel."* For a young person struggling to reclaim autonomy, that small moment of understanding can transform the dynamic from power struggle to partnership.

Validation lowers defenses and increases receptivity because it speaks directly to the nervous system's need for safety. When we feel misunderstood, our brain perceives threat; we defend, deny, or shut down. When we feel understood, even partially, our nervous system relaxes. The brain shifts from survival mode to engagement mode, and learning becomes possible.

Parents often fear that validation will make their loved one less accountable, but in practice, it does the opposite. People are far more likely to change once they feel seen. A young person who hears, *"You're not crazy for feeling this way,"* can finally stop fighting to prove their pain. That frees up energy for reflection and problem-solving. Without that foundation, even the most well-intentioned advice feels like criticism. Think of validation as emotional first aid. When someone is bleeding emotionally, your first job is not to analyze how they got hurt — it is to stop the bleeding. Validation does that. It stabilizes the emotional wound so that repair can begin. Once your loved one feels emotionally safe, you can address behavior, boundaries, and next steps. But until that moment of stabilization, logic rarely lands.

In recovery and mental health work, validation is what opens the door to accountability. Without it, people stay locked in cycles of shame and denial. Shame says, *"You're broken."* Validation says, *"You make sense."* And when someone feels they make sense, they can begin to make choices that also make sense. Accountability rooted in understanding leads to growth; accountability rooted in humiliation leads to resistance.

It is worth noting that validation works best when it is specific and authentic. Generic phrases like *"I understand how you feel"* can sound hollow if they're not backed by attunement. True validation reflects the emotional truth of the moment in your loved one's unique language. For example:

"You've been trying so hard to hold it together, and now it feels like no one notices."

"You feel like everything's spinning out of control, and this is the only way you can slow it down."

"You're frustrated because you want to be trusted, but you also don't trust yourself right now."

These reflections don't excuse behavior; they illuminate experience. They show your loved one that you're paying attention not just to what they're doing, but to what they're feeling. And when people feel accurately understood, they become more open to guidance, not less.

Validation also transforms the parent's experience. When you move from judging behavior to understanding the feeling beneath it, your own nervous system calms. You're no longer reacting from fear or anger; you're responding from empathy and stability. That regulation is contagious. Emotional steadiness in one person helps regulate the other. Over time, this creates a feedback loop of calm — what clinicians call co-regulation — in which both parent and loved one begin to communicate from a place of being grounded rather than from panic.

It is also important to remember that validation does not have to be verbal. It can be expressed through tone, eye contact, body language, or simply staying in the room when things get hard. A soft nod, a steady voice, or a hand on the shoulder communicates, *"I'm with you."* Those moments of quiet acknowledgment can be more powerful than any lecture.

In family systems work, we often say: *Understanding is not the same as agreeing.* You can understand the fear that led to substance use without approving of the choice. You can empathize with exhaustion without permitting withdrawal. You can validate the longing for independence while still setting firm limits. Validation is the bridge that allows those dual truths to coexist. At its core, validation is an act of dignity. It says to your loved one, *"You're not a problem to be solved — you're a person to be understood."*

That recognition alone can begin to restore the sense of worth that substance use and mental health struggles often erode. When people feel valued, they're more likely to value themselves. And when they value themselves, healing begins to take hold.

So when you find yourself in the familiar cycle — frustration rising, communication breaking down — pause and ask: *What is my loved one trying to tell me beneath these words? What emotion needs to be seen before this conversation can move forward?* That's where validation lives.

It does not mean saying, *"You're right."* It means saying, *"You make sense."*

And in a family healing from fear, shame, and chaos, that single message can be the most powerful intervention of all.

Come From a Place of Curiosity

Curiosity is communication's secret ingredient. It is what turns interrogation into exploration, and defensiveness into dialogue. In families navigating substance use or mental health challenges, curiosity is often the first skill to vanish and the most powerful one to reclaim. Fear narrows perspective; curiosity widens it. Judgment says, *"I already know what this means."* Curiosity says, *"I wonder what this means."* That small shift can transform the emotional climate of an entire conversation.

When a parent asks, *"Why would you lie about that?"* the underlying message — even if unintended — is accusation. It presumes wrongdoing and demands justification. The young person's brain, already wired to detect threat, interprets the question as danger. The amygdala fires, the body tenses, and the nervous system prepares to defend. Logic and reflection go offline. What you get in return is not honesty, but resistance: *"I don't know," "it is not a big deal," "You never listen anyway."* Now imagine a different approach: *"Help me understand what was happening when you decided not to tell me."* The content is similar — you're still addressing the lie — but the tone shifts completely. The phrase *help me understand* signals collaboration, not condemnation. It invites your loved one to explore their own behavior with you rather than against you. The brain interprets curiosity as safety. Defensiveness gives way to reflection. What could have been a confrontation becomes a conversation.

Curiosity communicates humility — the willingness to learn rather than assume. Adolescents and young adults, whose lives are often full of contradictions and uncertainty, respond to that humility with relief. It tells them that they don't have to be perfect to be in a relationship with you. That your love is big enough to hold complexity. And that they are safe enough to be honest.

Curiosity also helps parents regulate their own nervous systems. When you approach a hard conversation with judgment, your body enters a state of vigilance — you're looking for confirmation of danger, evidence of deception, proof of control lost. When you approach it with curiosity, you engage a different part of your brain — the one responsible for empathy, perspective, and problem-solving. Asking open-ended questions like, *"What was that like for you?"* or *"When did you first notice this starting to happen?"* not only helps your loved one reflect, but also helps *you* stay grounded. Curiosity and fear cannot co-exist in the same breath. Small linguistic shifts make a big difference. Phrases like *"help me understand," "what was that like,"* and *"when did you first notice"* transform the tone of communication. They signal openness rather than threat. They also slow the pace of the interaction, which gives the nervous system time to settle. In that slower rhythm, empathy becomes possible. The goal is not to in-terrogate for facts, but to explore for meaning.

When in doubt, start with the simplest phrase of all: *"Tell me more."* Those three words keep doors open. They say, *I'm listening. I'm not here to catch you; I'm here to know you.* In moments of tension, that single sentence can in-terrupt cycles of defensiveness and remind both of you that this relationship is bigger than the problem at hand.

Curiosity also allows for nuance — the understanding that behavior is often an expression of unmet need. A lie might be an attempt to avoid shame. A broken rule might be an experiment in autonomy. A harsh outburst might be a cover for grief. Judgment focuses on behavior in iso-lation; curiosity looks for the emotional logic underneath. When parents begin to see behavior as communication, empathy naturally follows. You start asking, *"What pain might this be protecting?"* rather than *"How could they do this to me?"*

It is important to note that curiosity does not mean ignoring boundaries or consequences. You can stay curious *and* hold limits. In fact, curiosity makes boundaries more effective because it reduces power struggles. When a young person feels heard, they're less likely to fight the boundary simply to prove their autonomy. You might say, *"I understand that staying out late feels important to you right now. I also need to know you're safe. Let's talk about what compromise might look like."* That balance — empathy with structure — is where real influence lives.

In recovery-oriented families, curiosity becomes a form of harm reduction. Instead of demanding total transparency or immediate change, you're building safety for gradual honesty. For example, a parent might say, *"I'd rather hear the truth, even if it is uncomfortable, than be in the dark. What would make it easier for you to tell me next time?"* That question shifts the focus from control to connection — from punishment to problem-solving. It acknowledges that honesty is hard when shame is high, and it invites the young person to participate in creating safer conditions for truth. Curiosity also models emotional maturity. It shows your loved one that it is possible to stay engaged in difficult conversations without collapsing into anger or avoidance. That modeling matters. Teens and young adults learn more from how you listen than from what you lecture. When you demonstrate curiosity, you're teaching them how to approach their own inner life with that same gentleness — how to ask themselves, *"Why did I feel the need to do that?"* instead of, *"What's wrong with me?"* Over time, that self-curiosity becomes the foundation for insight and growth.

Of course, staying curious isn't always easy. When fear takes over, curiosity feels like a luxury. In those moments, it can help to pause and literally breathe into the question: *"What else might be true here?"* That single thought can interrupt judgment before it hardens. It allows enough space for empathy to return. And that space — that half-second between reaction and response — is where healing begins.

When you lead with curiosity, you create a relational field where both people can be human — flawed, frightened, and still worthy of understanding. Curiosity does not erase accountability; it makes it possible. It shifts the goal of communication from being right to being real. It reminds everyone involved that this is not a courtroom but a relationship — one that can withstand difficult truths without collapsing. In the long arc of recovery and growth, curiosity is another bridge between survival and connection. It is the question mark that softens certainty, the open hand that replaces the pointing finger. It is the quiet invitation — *Tell me more* — that turns fear into conversation and conversation into healing.

Common Communication Traps

Even the most loving, well-intentioned parents fall into communication traps when they're scared. These patterns aren't signs of failure — they're reflexes born from urgency, love, and fear. When your loved one is struggling with substance use, mood swings, or mental health symptoms, every interaction can feel like a crisis. You want to help, to teach, to fix. But the very strategies that feel instinctive to you — explaining, persuading, reminding — are often the ones that push your loved one further away. Understanding these common traps isn't about blame; it is about awareness. When you can recognize what's happening in the moment, you have the power to shift the dynamic from escalation to connection.

Few communication patterns drain families more than the Lecture Loop — those long, impassioned speeches that begin with worry and end in frustration. Parents often enter the Lecture Loop when fear masquerades as logic. You've spent years trying to guide your loved one, and now you feel desperate for them to "get it." So you explain — again and again — why their choices are dangerous, how much you love them, what they're risking. The more anxious you become, the more words you use. But here's the hard truth: most teens and young adults stop listening after sentence three. Once a conversation turns into a monologue, their brain shifts into defense mode. They hear tone, not content. The words blur into background noise — another adult telling them what to do.

The irony is that lectures often come from love. You lecture because you care, because you want to protect. But long explanations rarely lead to insight; they lead to shut down. What your loved one needs isn't more information — it is less intensity. Try brevity and empathy instead. Replace, "You have to understand how serious this is..." with, "I know you're tired of hearing this, but I'm scared for you, and I want to figure this out together."

Short, emotionally honest statements land more effectively than long logical arguments. The key is tone, not length. When you can speak calmly and clearly — with fewer words and more heart — your message stands a better chance of getting through.

The Fix-It Reflex is one of the most common — and most loving — communication traps. it is the instinct to jump straight into problem-solving before your loved one's feelings have even been acknowledged. You hear distress and your brain immediately starts scanning for solutions: "Have you tried calling your therapist?" "Maybe you should take a break from that friend group." "We can sign you up for another activity." While well-intentioned, the Fix-It Reflex often backfires. When someone is overwhelmed, advice can feel like dismissal. Before a problem can be solved, it needs to be seen. Emotions must be processed before logic can take hold. When parents rush to fix, they inadvertently communicate, "Your feelings make me uncomfortable; let's move past them." That message — even when unintended — deepens isolation.

Start with presence before advice. Presence means holding space for the emotion, not the outcome. It can sound like, "That sounds really hard," or "I can tell how much this is weighing on you." Once your loved one feels seen, their nervous system calms — and their capacity for reflection returns. Only then can they truly hear your suggestions.

Remember: advice is effective only when the listener feels ready to receive it. Presence prepares that ground. Sometimes, the most powerful "fix" is silence paired with empathy.

Timing can make or break a conversation. Timing Mistakes often happen when emotions are high and patience is low — a difficult talk launched at 11 p.m., after a curfew violation, or in the middle of a crisis. Parents feel urgency: "We need to address this right now." But in those moments, both nervous systems are dysregulated. Neither of you is in a position to listen, much less learn. Difficult conversations require calm, predictable windows. Choose moments when both of you have the emotional bandwidth to stay grounded — not right before school, not during an argument, not in the heat of exhaustion. A helpful rule of thumb: if either person's heart rate is racing, it is not the right time.

You might say, "I want to talk about what happened, but it is late and we're both upset. Let's revisit this tomorrow." That simple act models emotional maturity. It shows that you value connection over control — and that conversations don't have to happen in chaos to matter. Parents sometimes worry that waiting sends the wrong message — that it means avoiding accountability. In reality, it teaches emotional regulation. It demonstrates that boundaries and reflection can coexist. Delaying the talk until both people are calm does not weaken the message;

it strengthens it. Because when emotions cool, empathy returns.

Perhaps the hardest communication trap to acknowledge — and the most transformative to address — is the Double Standard: expecting emotional control from your loved one when you are dysregulated yourself. Parents often demand calm from their loved one while communicating from their own state of panic or anger. It is an impossible paradox — one that young people feel instantly.

Adolescents and young adults are exquisitely attuned to tone, body language, and energy. When a parent says, "Calm down!" while visibly upset, the contradiction sends mixed signals. The message becomes, "Regulate for me, because I can't regulate for myself." But young people can't borrow calm that isn't being modeled. In family therapy, we often say, you can't ask for what you're not practicing. If you want your loved one to respond with openness, model openness. If you want them to take accountability, model accountability. If you want them to stay calm in conflict, show them what calm looks like in real time. This does not mean suppressing your emotions — it means managing them responsibly. You can say, "I'm upset right now, and I want to talk about this in a way that does not make things worse. I'm going to take a few minutes to settle down before we keep going." That is regulation in action.

When parents learn to model regulation, conversations become safer by default. The young person's nervous system senses, "This is different. I'm not being attacked."

Over time, that sense of safety rewires the relationship itself. The loved one begins to trust not just the parent's love, but their consistency. And consistency creates.

Each of these traps — the Lecture Loop, the Fix-It Reflex, Timing Mistakes, and Double Standards — is born from love. They are the strategies parents reach for when fear runs ahead of faith. The antidote is not perfection, but presence. When you find yourself slipping into one of these patterns, pause and take a breath. Ask yourself: What does this moment need — my control or my calm?

The answer is almost always the latter.

Communication that heals does not come from having the perfect words; it comes from having the right stance. A stance of curiosity, humility, and emotional steadiness. When you can offer those, even imperfectly, your words begin to matter again — not because they're flawless, but because they're felt.

Finding Your Regulated Voice

Every conversation has two nervous systems in it. One will lead. In moments of tension between parent and loved one, someone's emotional state will set the tone — and more often than not, it is the parents. The adult nervous system is the more developed one, capable of modulation, reflection, and pause. That means you hold the power to shape not only what is said, but how it is received. Here again is co-regulation — the process by which one person's calm can help another person's body find calm, too.

Before you speak, take a quiet moment to check in with yourself. Ask:

Is my goal to connect or to control?
Am I grounded enough to listen, not react?
Can I tolerate silence?

If the answer to any of these is no, pause. Step back. A short walk, a deep breath, or even a few minutes of stillness can save an entire dialogue. You're not avoiding the issue — you're preparing your nervous system to handle it effectively. When you enter a conversation from regulation rather than reactivity, your presence itself becomes a stabilizing force.

Many parents underestimate the physiological impact their emotional state has on the room. Our bodies communicate faster than our words. Tone, pacing, facial expression, and posture all transmit information before a single sentence is spoken. When your nervous system is agitated — heart racing, voice tight, muscles tense — your loved one's body senses it instantly. Their amygdala, the brain's alarm center, lights up in response, reading your energy as a potential threat. What follows is often misinterpreted as defiance or indifference, but in reality, it is self-protection. Conversely, when your body is calm, it sends the opposite message: *We're safe. We can think. We can talk.* The moment your breathing slows, your tone softens, and your body language opens, your loved one's nervous system begins to match that energy. This is co-regulation in action — biology doing what words alone cannot.

Think of yourself as the emotional thermostat of the home. When you lower your temperature, others follow. A steady presence does not just feel better — it creates the conditions for insight, trust, and change. It is not about suppressing your feelings; it is about stewarding them. There's a difference between *having emotions* and *being run by them.*

Finding your regulated voice means recognizing that timing matters as much as tone. Not every conversation needs to happen immediately. If you feel flooded — angry, scared, desperate — your brain is in survival mode. In that state, your capacity for empathy and flexibility is limited. You may speak sharply, overexplain, or raise your voice without meaning to. The impulse to "get it all out now" is a sign that your nervous system is seeking relief, not resolution. Relief feels urgent; resolution requires patience.

When you notice that urgency rising, pause and ground yourself before you continue. Try something physical: step outside, feel your feet on the ground, inhale through your nose for four counts and exhale for six. These small acts cue your parasympathetic nervous system — the body's built-in brake pedal — to slow down. Once your body calms, your words will follow. You can even name the pause aloud. Saying, *"I need a moment to collect my thoughts,"* models emotional regulation in real time. It shows your loved one that self-control isn't silence — it is responsibility. It tells them that emotions aren't dangerous, but they do need to be handled with care. This modeling teaches more than any lecture could.

The truth is, your calm is not just a gift to your loved one — it is a form of leadership. In families impacted by stress, anxiety, or addiction, chaos often becomes the baseline. Everyone is on alert, waiting for the next conflict or crisis. When you find your regulated voice, you interrupt that pattern. You say, through both word and presence: *We're not going to live in panic anymore.* That's how healing begins — not through control, but through steadiness. It is also important to remember that regulation is not perfection. You won't always stay composed, and that's okay. What matters most is how you repair after a rupture. If you lose your temper, own it. Say, *"I raised my voice because I got scared. That's on me. I'm going to try again."* That humility repairs trust faster than any justification ever could. Your loved one learns that accountability is part of love — that relationships can survive imperfection.

Over time, as you practice this awareness, you'll begin to notice subtle cues that tell you when you're slipping out of regulation. Maybe it is the tightening in your chest, the speed in your speech, or the urge to control the outcome. Those sensations aren't signs to push through — they're invitations to pause. The earlier you catch them, the less cleanup you'll have to do later.

Parents often say, *"But if I don't respond right away, I'll lose authority."* In truth, delayed response is a mark of authority. It shows discernment. Reactivity is impulsive; regulation is intentional. A regulated parent does not dominate — they anchor. They create a sense of safety that invites honesty, not fear.

There's an old saying in family therapy: *The calmest person in the room has the most influence.* It is true. Emotional energy flows toward the most stable source. If your loved one is spiraling and you join their chaos, the storm grows. If you stay steady, you become the grounding wire — the one safe point that helps discharge the emotional electricity. That steadiness is not passive; it is active containment. it is how you communicate, *You don't have to calm down alone. I can hold this with you.*

So before your next hard conversation, take a breath and ask yourself:

Is my voice grounded or gripping?
Am I trying to connect or to control?
Am I speaking to be heard, or to understand?

If you can answer with honesty, you'll know whether it is the right moment to speak — or to wait. And if you choose to wait, know that the pause itself is an act of care. It is not silence; it is preparation.

Finding your regulated voice isn't about becoming emotionless. It is about using your emotions wisely — as signals, not weapons. It is about remembering that in every hard moment, you have a choice: to match your loved one's chaos, or to model their way out of it. When you choose the latter, you become not just a parent, but a teacher of calm — a steady light in the fog, reminding everyone in the home that safety is possible, even here, even now.

Repairing after a Blow-Up

Even the most grounded, compassionate, and well-trained communicators lose it sometimes. You can practice regulation, validation, and curiosity all week, and then — one exhausting night, one sarcastic comment, one broken boundary — something inside of you snaps. You yell. You say something you regret. The conversation that started with good intentions ends with slammed doors, tears, or silence. This is not failure. It is family.

In recovery and mental health work, we often say that what heals relationships isn't perfection — it is *repair*. Perfection isn't realistic or even relational; it creates pressure, not safety. Repair, on the other hand, creates trust. It says, *we can rupture and come back.* That is the true definition of resilience — not avoiding conflict, but finding our way back to one another afterward. Conflict is inevitable in families under stress. What determines long-term health is not how often you argue, but how you reconnect afterward. Repair transforms tension into intimacy because it communicates three essential messages: *I see my impact, I care about your experience, and our relationship matters more than my pride.*

After a conflict, the first step is to take responsibility quickly. You don't have to craft the perfect apology or wait for the other person to calm down completely. A simple acknowledgment can reopen communication: *"I raised my voice; I wish I'd handled that differently."* Those few words carry enormous power. They demonstrate humility, accountability, and emotional intelligence — qualities that adolescents and young adults respect far more than authority alone. Notice that this statement does not overexplain. It does not justify or shift blame. It simply names the behavior. Responsibility without defense invites safety. It tells your loved one, *I'm not here to argue about who's right. I'm here to take ownership of my part.*

The second step is to name *impact,* not intention. Parents often rush to explain what they *meant — "I was just trying to help!" "I didn't mean to yell!" "You know how worried I am."* But in the aftermath of a blow-up, intention matters less than impact. Your loved one's nervous system experienced something — fear, hurt, rejection — and that experience needs acknowledgment before logic can land. You might say, *"I can see that scared you,"* or *"It looked like that really shut you down."* By naming impact, you validate their emotional reality. You're not confessing to being a "bad parent." You're saying, *"I see how my behavior affected you."* That recognition repairs what defensiveness can't. It restores dignity on both sides.

The third step is to reaffirm connection. After conflict, many young people worry — often silently — that the relationship has been damaged beyond repair. They wonder if their parent's anger means rejection, or if love is conditional. Reassurance helps rebuild that emotional safety net. Simple words like, *"We're okay. We'll figure this out,"* or *"I'm still here, even when we disagree,"* go a long way toward reestablishing stability. Reaffirming connection does not mean avoiding accountability or pretending the conflict didn't happen. It means reminding your loved one that disagreement and love can coexist — that hard moments don't erase belonging. This message is particularly crucial for teens and young adults dealing with shame, trauma, or substance use. Many already believe they are "too much," "too broken," or "too disappointing." When you stay connected after rupture, you challenge that internal narrative directly. You become living proof that they are still worthy of love, even in conflict.

Repair rewires trust faster than perfection ever could. Every time you return after tension — calmly, humbly, and consistently — you teach your loved one's nervous system that conflict isn't catastrophic. That lesson is especially healing in families where chaos, volatility, or avoidance have been the norm. Over time, these small acts of repair accumulate into emotional security. Your loved one learns, *"We can fight and still be safe."*

It is worth noting that repair does not have to happen immediately. Sometimes space is necessary. If emotions are still high, it is okay to wait until both nervous systems have settled. The key is to return. Even a day later, you can say, *"I've been thinking about our conversation, and I realize I could have handled that better."* Late repair is still repair. It signals reflection and care.

Humility is the foundation of all repairs. It takes courage to admit imperfection, especially when you're the parent — the one who's supposed to have it together. But humility does not weaken authority; it strengthens it. When you take responsibility, you model accountability. You show your loved one that strength and softness can coexist — that being an adult isn't about being right all the time, but about owning your mistakes and making them right.

Consistency is equally important. One apology can open a door, but repeated repair builds trust. Each time you follow through, your loved one learns that emotional safety with you is not a one-time event — it is a pattern. This reliability helps counter the unpredictability that often accompanies mental health struggles or substance use in the family system.

Repair is not a performance. It is a practice. It is not about using the "right" therapeutic language or following a script. It is about authenticity. If you're still learning how to stay calm, admit that. If you feel unsure, say so. What matters most is your sincerity. Teens and young adults can sense authenticity immediately — and they respond to it far more than to perfection.

In recovery work, consistency and humility outweigh flawless technique. Families don't heal because everyone starts communicating perfectly; they heal because people keep trying. Every apology, every reconnection, every moment of calm after chaos is a neural rehearsal for safety.

The brain learns through repetition: *Conflict happens. Repair follows. Love remains.*

So when the next blow-up happens— take a breath. Step back, not away. Then return with humility and care. Say, *"That got heated. I don't like how I handled it, and I want to try again."* At that moment, you are doing more than repairing a conversation. You are rewiring your family's sense of safety. You are teaching your loved one that rupture is survivable, and that love is durable enough to withstand real life.

That's the work of healing — not flawless communication, but faithful return.

Family Roles in Communication

In families navigating substance use or mental health challenges, communication does not happen in a vacuum — it unfolds within a system. Every member of that system develops patterns, often unconsciously, to manage stress, fear, and uncertainty. These patterns are not character flaws; they are coping mechanisms. Each role evolved at some point to maintain balance, reduce conflict, or create predictability when life felt unpredictable.

When a loved one is struggling, family members instinctively step into positions meant to restore stability — but those same positions can end up reinforcing disconnection. The more stress a family is under, the more rigidly everyone plays their part. Communication becomes less about understanding and more about maintaining equilibrium, even if that equilibrium is painful. Recognizing your own role in the system isn't about blame; it is about awareness. Awareness creates choice — the freedom to respond differently rather than react automatically. The goal is not to erase these roles but to *soften* them, to make room for authenticity instead of performance.

Below are some of the most common communication roles that appear in families under stress.

The Fixer

The Fixer is the emotional first responder of the family — the one who jumps in to solve problems, soothe conflict, and restore calm. Their heart is almost always in the right place. They love deeply, worry constantly, and feel responsible for everyone else's stability. When things start to unravel, the Fixer goes into overdrive: sending reminders, scheduling appointments, suggesting solutions, and trying to talk everyone back to reason. But the Fixer's strength — their ability to act — can also become their trap. In their effort to hold everything together, they often take on more responsibility than is theirs to hold. They might unintentionally interrupt others' emotional processing or rescue people from the natural consequences of their choices. Over time, this can lead to exhaustion, resentment, or a sense that no one else is trying as hard.

The Fixer's challenge is to remember that care and control are not the same thing. True healing requires space for discomfort. The Fixer can learn to pause before responding, to ask, *"What am I feeling right now, and whose emotion am I trying to manage?"* Sometimes, the most loving action is inaction — letting others find their footing while offering steady support from the sidelines.

The Avoider

The Avoider is the peacekeeper — the one who stays quiet, changes the subject, or minimizes tension to keep the family from exploding. Avoiders often grew up in homes where conflict felt unsafe, so silence became a form of protection. They believe that calm equals safety, even if that calm is built on suppression rather than resolution. In moments of stress, the Avoider might say, *"Let's not talk about it right now,"* or simply leave the room. They tend to prioritize harmony over honesty and may secretly hope that if enough time passes, problems will resolve themselves. But unspoken tension does not dissolve — it festers. Avoidance keeps peace in the short term but creates distance in the long term.

The Avoider's strength — their sensitivity to emotional tone — can become a tool for healing when paired with courage. Learning to stay in discomfort without fleeing is their growth edge. They can practice saying things like, *"This is hard for me to talk about, but I want to try,"* or *"I get quiet when things feel tense, but I care about what's happening."* Naming the avoidance out loud transforms it into awareness.

The Enforcer

The Enforcer values order, structure, and rules. When the family system feels chaotic, they rely on control to create predictability. Their logic is simple: if everyone would just follow the plan, things wouldn't fall apart. They set boundaries firmly, often out of love, but their tone can come across as rigid or punitive. The Enforcer feels safest when others behave. This role often develops in parents who have experienced fear or helplessness. Control becomes their way of fighting back against anxiety. But strictness without connection can alienate rather than protect. Teens and young adults interpret the Enforcer's structure as mistrust or rejection, and communication shuts down.

The Enforcer's work is to soften structure with empathy. They can still hold clear boundaries — in fact, families need them — but those boundaries must be paired with understanding. The shift might sound like, *"I can't allow this behavior because I care about your safety,"* instead of, *"You broke the rules, so now you're grounded."* Rules enforced with compassion become guidance rather than punishment.

The Enforcer's strength is clarity; their growth lies in flexibility. True authority isn't about control — it is about steadiness. When the Enforcer learns to regulate their own fear, they become not the disciplinarian of the home, but its anchor.

The Mediator

The Mediator serves as the emotional translator — the bridge between family members who can't seem to hear each other. They might be a parent caught between partners, a sibling caught between parents and loved one, or even the adolescent themselves trying to smooth the tension between the adults. Mediators absorb conflict to keep relationships intact. The Mediator often says things like, *"They didn't mean it that way,"* or *"Let me talk to them for you."* They're empathic, diplomatic, and highly attuned to everyone else's needs. But the emotional labor of constant translation comes at a cost. Mediators often neglect their own feelings, fearing that expressing them will disrupt the fragile balance they have been maintaining. Over time, they can feel invisible — valued for their peacekeeping but rarely seen for their own pain.

The Mediator's strength is empathy; their challenge is boundaries. Healing begins when they step out of the middle and let others hold their own discomfort. it is okay to say, *"I care about both of you, but I can't be the go-between anymore."* That single sentence can release enormous emotional tension from the system. When the Mediator stops over-functioning, others are invited to grow.

Moving from Roles to Relationships

Recognizing these roles is the first step toward change. Most families contain elements of all four — sometimes within the same person. You might be a Fixer at work, an Avoider with your partner, and an Enforcer with your loved one. Roles shift depending on stress level and context. The key is noticing when you've slipped into a reactive pattern. Awareness creates pause, and pause creates possibility. When you can say, *"I'm in my Fixer mode right now,"* or *"I'm avoiding because I'm scared of conflict,"* you shift from acting out the role to observing it. That small bit of distance gives you the power to choose differently. The goal isn't to eliminate these parts of yourself — they developed for good reasons. Each role carries wisdom: the Fixer's compassion, the Avoider's sensitivity, the Enforcer's clarity, the Mediator's empathy. Healing communication means keeping the wisdom while releasing the rigidity.

When families soften their roles, conversations become more authentic. The Fixer learns to listen without solving. The Avoider learns to speak even when it is uncomfortable. The Enforcer learns to set limits without losing warmth. The Mediator learns to step back and trust others to find their own voice. This process takes practice and patience. Patterns that have been in place for years won't shift overnight. But every small moment of awareness — every time you choose presence over performance — moves the family closer to balance.

In recovery work, this is what growth looks like: not perfect communication, but *pattern recognition with compassion*. When you can see the system clearly, you stop fighting it blindly. You begin to replace reactivity with intention — and that is where genuine connection begins.

When Your Teen or Young Adult Won't Talk

Few experiences are more painful for a parent than trying to connect with a loved one who has gone quiet. The silence can feel like a wall — heavy, opaque, and full of meaning you can't quite reach. You ask questions and get one-word answers. You offer comfort and are met with shrugs. Sometimes the silence lasts hours; sometimes it stretches for weeks. Parents often describe it as "losing" their loved one while they're still right in front of them. It is natural to interpret that silence as rejection. But silence, especially in adolescents and young adults navigating mental health or substance use challenges, is almost never about indifference. Silence is communication. It often says, *"I don't trust that this will go well."* Or *"I'm afraid of being judged, lectured, or misunderstood."* Or even, *"I don't know what I feel yet."*

Your job as a parent is not to force the words out, but to prove — gently, repeatedly — that conversation with you can feel safe. That it won't always end in conflict or correction. That it is okay to be uncertain, quiet, or even resistant, and that the relationship can hold all of that without shattering. When your loved one shuts down, the instinct is to push harder — to fill the silence, to demand answers, to remind them how worried you are. These impulses come from love, but to a dysregulated or overwhelmed young person, they can feel like intrusion. The more you push, the tighter they close. The goal, instead, is to reduce pressure while maintaining presence.

Connection does not always happen in deep, heart-to-heart conversations. Often, it happens in micro-moments — small, seemingly ordinary interactions that slowly rebuild trust. A car ride where you talk about nothing important. Folding laundry together in a comfortable quiet. Sharing a snack or watching a show without commentary. These moments communicate: *I'm still here. We don't have to fix anything right now. We can just be.* When conversation feels impossible, shift your focus from *talking* to *being with.* Connection begins in shared calm, not shared words. The nervous system registers safety long before the mind articulates it. If your presence feels nonthreatening and predictable, your teen's or young adult's guard will gradually lower.

Sometimes, naming the silence directly — but gently — can be powerful. You might say, *"I notice it has been hard to talk lately. I don't want to push, but I'm here when you're ready."* This simple acknowledgment plants a seed of safety. It tells your loved one, *"I see what's happening, and I can tolerate it."* For many young people, especially those who've experienced conflict around communication, that message alone is healing. It proves that the relationship can survive discomfort — that love does not require constant dialogue to exist.

The key is tone. This is not an invitation wrapped in guilt, *"you never talk to me anymore!"* or control, *"you need to start opening up."*. It is a statement of steadiness. It says, *"I'm available, not demanding."* The more consistently you can hold that tone — curious, calm, non-intrusive — the more your loved one begins to believe that it is safe to re-engage. It is also important to understand that silence often masks ambivalence. Teens and young adults in recovery or distress may desperately want connection but fear the vulnerability it requires. They test safety through withdrawal: *If I pull away, will they chase me, or will they stay calm?* Your consistent presence during these tests teaches them that you can handle distance without punishment or panic.

When words do come, resist the urge to reward disclosure with overreaction. Parents sometimes meet the first hint of openness with too much intensity — advice, emotion, or relief — which can make the young person retreat again. Instead, stay grounded. Listen more than you speak. A simple *"Thank you for telling me that"* is often enough. It shows you can hold their truth without judgment or overwhelm.

You can also use parallel activities to invite communication indirectly. Conversations flow more easily when there's no direct eye contact or formal setup. Car rides, walks, cooking together, or working side by side often create the right balance of connection and space. Movement calms the nervous system; shared tasks lower the social pressure. Many adolescents open up not when asked questions, but when they sense quiet companionship.

If the silence feels prolonged or worrisome — lasting weeks or deepening into isolation — it may help to seek family therapy or parent consultation. A neutral professional can help decode what's beneath the withdrawal and guide both sides back toward safe communication. But even then, your role remains the same: to embody steadiness. Therapy works best when it is paired with consistent emotional safety at home. It is also worth remembering that silence does not mean nothing is happening. Often, internal processing is taking place beneath the surface. The young person may be sorting through shame, confusion, or exhaustion. They may not yet have the language for what they're feeling. Pushing for conversation before they're ready can interrupt that inner work. Your restraint allows it to unfold.

In family systems terms, this is the difference between pressure and presence. Pressure demands change now; presence communicates faith that change is possible. When you shift from *"We need to talk"* to *"I'm here whenever you're ready,"* you remove urgency from the relationship and replace it with trust. Trust takes time, but it grows best in consistency.

Over time, you may notice small openings — a question, a comment, a sigh that lingers instead of deflects. These are invitations. Respond lightly. Meet them where they are, not where you wish they'd be. The goal is not a long conversation; it is a moment of connection. Every small success reinforces the message: *This is safe.*

Silence is not the enemy of connection. It is part of the process. In recovery work, silence often precedes honesty — a space where defenses melt just enough for truth to begin forming. When you treat silence not as defiance but as data — information about safety, readiness, or overwhelm — you transform frustration into insight. And when you meet that silence with steadiness rather than fear, you teach the most powerful lesson of all: that love does not demand words to be real. That you can hold space, calmly and patiently, while someone finds their way back to speech.

Because in the end, connection isn't built on perfect timing or constant talking. it is built on the quiet confidence that no matter how many pauses there are, the relationship remains — solid, safe, and waiting with open arms when the words return.

Practical Tools for Connection

1. Use "AND" instead of "BUT."

"I know you're frustrated, *and* we still need to talk about safety." Replacing these words allows acknowledgment instead of erasing the validating statement.

2. Set boundaries with warmth.

"I can't allow substances in the house, *and* I love you unconditionally." As we will discuss in Chapter 4, boundaries can be difficult for the recipient to process. However, delivering boundaries with warmth and love makes them feel safer for the recipient to navigate.

3. Mirror and summarize.

"What I'm hearing is that you felt trapped at school today." Helping your teen or young adult feel heard and validated will bring the sense of safety and empowerment needed to calm their nervous system and create connection.

4. Pause before responding.

A two-second breath changes outcomes. It may feel like an eternity to you in certain situations, but that pause can shift the tone and outcome of the conversation.

5. End on connection.

No matter the conflict, close with: "I love you. We'll keep working on this." One of the hardest obstacles for a teen or young adult who is struggling is the feeling of isolation and aloneness in their struggle. Maintaining that connection is essential for positive outcomes.

The Parent's Inner Dialogue

Behind every tense conversation is a parent's inner world — a swirl of thoughts and feelings that rarely get spoken aloud. Beneath the surface of advice, frustration, or pleading lies something much more vulnerable: fear. Fear of losing your loved one. Fear of saying the wrong thing. Fear that the situation will never get better. Even if those words never cross your lips, your loved one can feel them in your tone, your pauses, your urgency.

When communication breaks down, parents often assume the problem lies only in what's being said. But much of what shapes a conversation lives in what's *felt.* The energy beneath your words speaks louder than the content. A calm statement delivered through tension will sound anxious. A gentle question layered with fear will feel intrusive. Your nervous system — your tone, breathing, and pacing — becomes part of the message. It is natural to feel scared. Parenting through crisis asks the impossible: to stay connected to someone whose behavior may frighten or confuse you. You may find yourself oscillating between extremes — wanting to hold tighter, then realizing you must let go, feeling compassion one moment and resentment the next. These inner shifts are not signs of weakness; they are signs of love meeting uncertainty.

Before you enter a difficult conversation, take a moment to ground yourself. Regulation always begins with awareness. Ask yourself: *What's happening to me right now? What emotion am I bringing into this room?* If the answer is fear, shame, anger, or despair, pause. Those emotions are understandable — but if they go unacknowledged, they will drive your tone.

A helpful way to prepare is to write down your intention in one sentence. Something simple and clear. For example:

I want to understand what they're feeling, not fix it.
I want to communicate care, even if we disagree.
I want to hold a boundary without shame or anger.

This small act externalizes your purpose and helps you stay anchored when emotions rise. During the conversation, you can silently return to that sentence as a compass: *Is what I'm saying aligned with my intention? Or am I speaking from panic?*

Then, imagine speaking from compassion rather than fear. Visualization is not just a mindfulness exercise; it is neuroscience in action. When you picture yourself responding calmly, your brain begins rehearsing that state. The next time conflict arises, your nervous system will recognize it more easily. You're literally building neural pathways for steadiness. It can also help to remember that your loved one's behavior — however distressing — is *information,* not a verdict on your parenting. When a teen or young adult struggles with substance use, emotional dysregulation, or mental health challenges, parents often internalize blame. You might think, *If I had done something differently, this wouldn't be happening.* But behavior is communication, not condemnation. It is a signal about pain, need, or overwhelm — not evidence that you failed.

When you see your loved one's behavior as data instead of judgment, you can respond with curiosity rather than shame. Instead of *"What did I do wrong?"* you can ask, *"What might this be trying to tell me?"* That shift in internal dialogue transforms your stance from reactive to reflective. It restores your ability to lead with empathy rather than guilt.

It is also worth noticing how fear shapes the *timing* and *tone* of your communication. Fear makes us rush. It shortens patience and speeds up speech. You can feel it in your own body — the tightness in your chest, the urge to talk faster, the pressure to get through to them right now. But urgency, even when born from love, feels like pressure to someone who's already overwhelmed. When you notice that urgency rising, pause for one deep breath before speaking. It sounds simple, but physiologically it changes everything. A single slow exhale activates the parasympathetic nervous system — the body's calming mechanism. You can even place your hand on your chest or your stomach to signal to your body: *We're okay. This isn't an emergency.* You're not just calming yourself; you're communicating calm to your loved one through your very presence.

Parenting through crisis asks you to hold two truths at once — truths that can feel contradictory but are equally real:

1. You cannot control the outcome.
2. Your presence still matters profoundly.

These truths are the twin pillars of compassionate parenting. The first calls for surrender; the second calls for engagement. Together, they create balance.

You cannot control whether your loved one accepts help, changes behavior, or finds recovery on your timeline. Trying to control those things leads to burnout and resentment. But your presence — your willingness to stay connected without rescuing, to stay calm without withdrawing — can change everything. Presence communicates safety, and safety is what opens the door to healing. Sometimes, your inner dialogue will sound like a tug-of-war between these two truths: *I need to do something* and *I can't fix this.* The challenge is not to silence that tension, but to live inside it with compassion. To say to yourself, *I can love them fiercely and still recognize my limits. I can care deeply without collapsing under responsibility that isn't mine.*

It helps to have compassion not only for your loved one, but for yourself. Parenting a struggling young person is profoundly disorienting. You're asked to be both a caregiver and a boundary-setter, to show empathy while enforcing limits, to remain hopeful without slipping into denial. That is complex emotional labor. Expecting yourself to do it perfectly is unrealistic — and unnecessary. What your loved one needs most is not a perfect parent, but a regulated one.

When you ground yourself before big conversations, you create space for that regulation to grow. You stop reacting from the scared voice that says, *"I'm losing them,"* and start responding from the steadier one that says, *"They're struggling, and I can meet this moment with calm."* Over time, that steadiness becomes the emotional foundation your loved one leans on when they're ready.

Even in silence, your grounded presence speaks. It says: *I'm here. I'm listening. I can hold both our fear and our hope.*

Because ultimately, the work of parenting through crisis is not about controlling outcomes — it is about communicating safety through presence. It is about letting your loved one feel, in their bones, that no matter how chaotic things get, they are not navigating it alone.

And it starts not with what you say to them, but with what you say to yourself.

When to Seek Professional Support

There comes a point in some families when every conversation seems to circle back to the same painful place — either erupting into conflict or dissolving into silence. You try to stay calm, to use everything you've learned about regulation, curiosity, and connection. But somehow, the pattern repeats. Words become triggers instead of bridges. Even the most well-intentioned talk feels like walking on eggshells.

When that happens, it is time to widen the circle of support.

Inviting a neutral professional into your family's process isn't a sign of weakness — it is a sign of strength. It means you recognize that communication has become too charged to manage alone and that a skilled guide can help your family learn a new way of relating. Family therapy, parent coaching, or work with a clinician trained in adolescent and young adult systems can create a structured space for understanding, healing, and practice. If every conversation ends in escalation or withdrawal, it is not because your family is "broken." It is because your nervous systems are exhausted. When fear, frustration, and misunderstanding pile up over time, communication becomes survival driven. Everyone is speaking from their most defensive parts. A neutral professional helps slow that process down. They model how to pause, how to translate, and how to repair.

Professionals trained in family systems work do more than mediate arguments — they interpret patterns. They listen not only to what's being said, but how it is being said, and what emotional needs might be hiding beneath the words. When a parent says, *"You never tell me what's going on,"* the therapist might hear, *"I feel scared and shut out."* When a teen says, *"You don't get it,"* the therapist might help them reframe that into, *"I need you to listen without fixing."*

In this sense, family therapy is less about blame and more about language rehabilitation. You're learning a new dialect together — one based on emotional accuracy, mutual respect, and repair. The therapist becomes a kind of interpreter between nervous systems, helping each person articulate what they truly mean instead of what fear or frustration makes them say. The right professional can also help identify when communication struggles are symptoms of something deeper — such as anxiety, depression, trauma, or substance use — and ensure those issues are treated appropriately. Sometimes what looks like "defiance" or "manipulation" is actually avoidance rooted in fear or shame. A skilled clinician can help reframe behavior in a way that invites compassion without excusing harm.

For parents, professional support also provides something equally important: a place to process your own emotions. When you're constantly managing crises or walking on eggshells, you can lose sight of your own needs. A therapist or parent coach can help you untangle guilt from responsibility, love from control, and hope from denial. They can help you discern when to lean in, when to set limits, and when to let natural consequences unfold.

Sometimes parents hesitate to seek help because they fear judgment — from professionals, friends, or even themselves. The belief that "good families should handle things privately" runs deep. But healing does not happen in isolation. Complex problems require relational solutions. You're not admitting failure by asking for help;

you're modeling resilience. You're showing your loved one that seeking guidance is part of healthy adulthood.

It can help to think of therapy as a form of coaching. Just as an athlete brings in a trainer to improve performance, families bring in therapists to strengthen communication and teamwork. The therapist does not "fix" anyone; they teach you new skills, create structure for hard conversations, and provide feedback in real time. They help your family move from reacting to relating.

Different types of professional support can meet different needs:

Family Therapy focuses on the dynamics among all family members. it is especially effective when communication patterns are entrenched or when substance use, mental health symptoms, or major transitions are affecting everyone.

Parent Coaching offers individualized guidance for caregivers — helping you refine your communication strategies, set appropriate boundaries, and manage your own emotional responses.

Individual Therapy for parents or teens provides a safe space to process private feelings that might otherwise spill into family interactions.

Group Support for parents or families can normalize your experience. Hearing others share similar struggles can reduce shame and foster community.

No matter which path you choose, the goal is the same: to create safety — both emotional and relational. A good therapist helps each person in the family feel seen, heard, and capable of change. They teach practical communication scripts tailored to your family's patterns. For example, they might help a parent shift from *"You're being disrespectful,"* to *"When you walk away mid-conversation, I feel dismissed and worried."* Or they might help a teen move from *"You're always on my case,"* to *"I feel overwhelmed when you check in so often."* Over time, these micro-adjustments transform how families talk to one another. The home slowly becomes less reactive and more reflective — a place where honesty does not have to mean hostility.

The therapeutic space also serves as a rehearsal studio for communication. You get to practice new ways of speaking in real time, with feedback and guidance. Mistakes are expected and welcomed. The therapist's role is to keep the environment safe enough for trial and error — because every family learns through experimentation.

For many parents, this process is a relief. It means you no longer have to hold every conversation alone. You can share that responsibility with someone trained to keep things constructive. It also takes pressure off your relationship with your loved one, allowing you to return to being a parent rather than a perpetual negotiator or crisis manager.

When you seek professional support, you're not outsourcing love — you're enhancing it. You're inviting an ally into your family's system who can help you rebuild communication on stronger, calmer ground. And just as importantly, you're showing your loved one that growth does not mean perfection — it means knowing when to ask for help.

Because in the end, the goal isn't to talk *better* just for the sake of smoother communication. it is to create a family environment where honesty feels safe, vulnerability is possible, and everyone — parent and loved one alike — feels free to speak in their truest voice.

Small Successes Count

In the early stages of rebuilding trust and communication, progress often whispers rather than announces itself. Parents frequently imagine that healing will look like transformation — open conversations, changed behavior, visible breakthroughs. But most healing begins quietly. It looks like ordinary moments that used to end badly now ending differently.

A conversation that ends without shouting.

A door that stays open, or closes quietly, instead of slamming.

A teen or young adult who texts you first, even about something small.

A shared laugh in the middle of an argument.

A moment of humor after tension that once would have spiraled out of control.

These are not small things. They are the first, fragile signs of healing in motion.

Progress rarely feels like progress when you're living it. It often feels like exhaustion — like one step forward, one step back. But change, especially in families navigating recovery or emotional turmoil, unfolds gradually. The nervous system does not rewrite itself overnight. It learns safety in micro-moments — short, repeated experiences of calm, repair, and connection. Every time you and your loved one move through a hard moment differently than before, you're building new neural pathways together.

You can think of these moments as *emotional repetitions.* Just as physical strength is built through consistent small movements, relational strength is built through consistent small interactions. Each time a conversation ends without escalation, the brain learns: *We can survive conflict.* Each time your teen or young adult initiates contact, their nervous system is testing: *Is it safe to reconnect?* And each time you respond with calm instead of control, your system replies: *Yes, it is safe.* Because the process is so incremental, it is easy to miss or minimize these moments. Many parents look for "big change" — total honesty, sustained sobriety, a dramatic shift in attitude. When those larger milestones take time to appear, it can feel discouraging. But transformation is made up of tiny, consistent interactions that accumulate quietly until one day they become visible.

That's why it is vital to celebrate progress aloud. When you notice a moment that feels different — more open, less tense, more genuine — name it gently and with sincerity. You might say:

"I appreciated how honest you were just now."

"Thanks for sticking with this conversation even though it was hard."

"That was a tough moment, and I'm proud of how we both handled it."

These acknowledgments matter far more than they seem. For your teen or young adult, they provide feedback that safety and effort are noticed — and that progress, however small, is valued. For you, they reinforce mindfulness, helping you stay attuned to growth instead of only scanning for problems.

Positive reinforcement is one of the most powerful tools in parenting, not because it manipulates behavior, but because it strengthens connection. What you notice, you nurture. Neuroscience shows that the brain is shaped more effectively by encouragement than by correction. When we highlight what's working, we activate the brain's reward pathways, releasing dopamine and reinforcing the behaviors we hope to see again. In contrast, chronic focus on mistakes triggers shame, defensiveness, and withdrawal — the very states that make communication harder.

This does not mean you ignore boundaries or avoid hard conversations. It means you balance them with acknowledgment and warmth. For example, after a difficult talk about curfews or substance use, you might end by saying, *"That wasn't an easy conversation, but I really appreciate how you stayed with me through it."* That simple statement transforms what could feel punitive into something collaborative. It communicates: *We're in this together.*

Celebrating small progress also protects hope — and hope is the emotional oxygen of family recovery. When days feel long and setbacks happen, remembering even a few bright moments keeps you from slipping into despair. Hope isn't about denial; it is about perspective. It is the quiet voice that says, *"We're still moving, even if it is slow."* If you find it difficult to see progress, try keeping a brief reflection journal. Once a week, jot down one small moment of connection, however fleeting. It might be as simple as your loved one accepting a ride, saying goodnight, or offering a small smile after an argument. Over time, reading back through these notes can reveal how far you've come. Healing rarely feels linear in the moment, but looking backward often shows you the arc.

Another practice is to share your sense of progress with your loved one, when appropriate. Teens and young adults often believe parents only notice what goes wrong. When you name what's going right, you interrupt that belief. You show that you see them as more than their struggles.

And remember: progress belongs to everyone in the family. it is not just about your loved one's change — it is about yours too. When you stay calm in moments that used to trigger you, when you listen instead of lecture, when you take a pause instead of reacting — that's growth. You're rewiring your own nervous system to respond differently, modeling the very regulation you hope to see in your loved one.

There's a quiet dignity in this kind of progress. It does not make headlines, but it changes the atmosphere of a home. One less argument this week. One more shared meal. One softer goodbye. These moments are the architecture of trust being rebuilt brick by brick. Progress isn't always visible to outsiders — but you'll feel it in the rhythm of your home. Fewer slammed doors. More eye contact. Quicker recovery after tension. These are the vital signs of healing.

Over time, these subtle improvements accumulate until one day you notice something startlingly ordinary: a peaceful afternoon, a calm dinner, laughter you didn't have to force. That's the reward for all the unseen work — the thousands of quiet choices to stay present, breathe, and try again. Healing in families is rarely dramatic. It is humble, repetitive, and rooted in the everyday. But it is also incredibly powerful. Every small moment of calm connection tells your loved one — and your own nervous system — that safety is possible again.

So when progress comes softly, let yourself recognize it. Name it. Celebrate it. Because these are not small things. They are the living proof that change is happening — one quiet, courageous moment at a time.

Reflection Exercise: Your Communication Inventory

1. What topics create the most reactivity between us?
2. How do I typically respond when I feel scared or powerless?
3. What does my loved one need to feel safe talking to me?
4. When was a time we communicated well—what was different then?
5. What's one habit I can change this week that would make our talks calmer?

What to Expect as Communication Heals

When you begin to change the way you communicate — softening your tone, pausing instead of reacting, replacing lectures with listening — it can feel like nothing is working. You're putting in effort, but the other side of the conversation may not yet be responding the way you hope. You try to stay calm, and your teen rolls their eyes. You ask a curious question, and they say, *"Oh great, now you're trying therapist talk."*

That's okay. It is normal.

When you start using new communication skills, don't expect fireworks. Expect skepticism. Expect testing. Your loved one needs to know if this new version of you is real or just another phase. For years, their nervous system has been conditioned to expect a certain response — maybe defensiveness, anger, or withdrawal. When you suddenly respond differently, it can actually feel unsettling at first. Change, even positive change, takes time to trust.

Consistency, not perfection, wins credibility.

The goal isn't to get it "right" every time. it is to keep returning to calm, to curiosity, to compassion — even when conversations go sideways. When your loved one pushes back, it is not proof that your efforts are failing; it is evidence that they're noticing. Testing boundaries is part of rebuilding trust. Your steadiness in those moments sends a powerful message: *This is different now. I can handle this without exploding or withdrawing.* Over time — often weeks or months — you'll start to notice small but unmistakable shifts. The atmosphere in your home begins to soften. The tension that once filled every silence starts to ease. Arguments that used to escalate for hours now lose steam more quickly. You may catch glimpses of humor returning — a shared smile, a quiet joke, a spark of familiarity in the middle of all the uncertainty. These are signs of healing.

Communication slowly becomes less about convincing and more about understanding. Instead of trying to make your point or get the last word, you begin listening for what's underneath the words being said. You stop needing to win, and you start wanting to connect. That subtle change in intention transforms the entire emotional climate of a household. When understanding becomes the goal, defensiveness fades. This shift — from control to connection, from fixing to listening — can stabilize even a home in crisis. It does not erase problems, but it creates a foundation sturdy enough to hold them. A family that can communicate calmly can navigate almost anything. A family that can't talk without chaos is always on edge, no matter how much love there is.

When you communicate differently, you are not only changing words — you are changing energy. Tone, pace, and presence all contribute to the nervous system's sense of safety. When you stay steady, your teen's or young adult's brain gradually learns that it does not have to stay in defense mode. Over time, safety leads to openness, and openness leads to honesty. This process is invisible at first, but it is how real transformation happens.

As communication heals, it is important to remember that progress rarely feels linear. Some weeks, things will feel lighter — more laughter, less tension — and then something will trigger an old pattern, and the air will thicken again. That's normal too. Healing does not mean never slipping back into old habits; it means recovering from them faster. What once took days of silence may now take an hour. That's growth. In these moments, try to zoom out. Instead of measuring success by the absence of conflict, measure it by the speed of repair. Notice how long it takes to return to calm after a disagreement. Notice if your loved one comes back to you more quickly. These small indicators tell you that communication is becoming safer on both sides.

You cannot control your adolescent or young adult's recovery, but you can influence the climate in which it unfolds. Think of communication as the weather system of the home. You can't control whether it rains, but you can help determine whether the house has shelter, warmth, and light. The way you speak — the tone you set, the steadiness you bring — shapes the emotional atmosphere your loved one lives in.

Communication that connects does not demand — it invites. It does not rescue — it respects. It transforms the home from a battlefield into a landing pad. That transformation does not happen in a single conversation; it happens over hundreds of small, imperfect ones. Each attempt at understanding builds another layer of trust. In the storm of addiction, anxiety, depression, or any co-occurring challenge, words are not just tools; they're lights. Each calm sentence, each listening moment, each repaired conversation adds wattage to your family's searchlight — illuminating the path forward, even when visibility is low. The light may not banish the storm immediately, but it keeps everyone oriented toward safety.

Eventually, you'll start to feel a quiet shift — the moment when communication no longer feels like a constant test, but like a shared rhythm. Conversations may still be hard, but they no longer carry the same level of threat. You both begin to trust that conflict does not mean collapse. This is one of the greatest gifts of family healing: the ability to disagree and stay connected.

As communication improves, you may also notice subtle emotional changes in yourself. You begin reacting less and reflecting more. You become less afraid of silence. You realize that your calmness does not depend on your loved one's mood. You learn to trust your own capacity to hold difficult feelings without losing yourself. This self-trust is the foundation of resilient parenting — and of genuine connection. One day, maybe without even realizing it, you'll find yourself in a moment that would once have spiraled — and instead, it passes quietly. You stay grounded. Your teen shrugs, mutters something, and walks away — and you don't chase. Later, they wander back in, sit down, and start talking about something unrelated. That's the miracle of slow healing: it sneaks up on you in ordinary moments.

These changes won't always be visible from the outside. Outsiders may still see a family in process. But you'll know the truth — that beneath the surface, something essential has shifted. The current is flowing differently now. Every small change in communication is cumulative. Each moment of calm builds on the last. Each repair strengthens the bridge. And even when the larger journey of recovery feels uncertain, these small relational wins are evidence that healing is underway — not only in your loved one, but in your family system as a whole.

So when you doubt yourself, when progress feels invisible or too slow, remember: you are teaching your family a new language — one built on steadiness, respect, and love that does not disappear under pressure. That language will outlast the storm.

In the end, communication isn't about mastering the right words; it is about embodying safety. it is about becoming the quiet, steady light that guides everyone — including yourself — back home.

Chapter 4

Boundaries That Heal, Not Harm

Parents often approach boundaries with a mixture of dread and guilt. They know structure is important but fear that setting limits will drive their loved one away. When a young person is struggling with substance use or emotional instability, every rule feels like a potential explosion. Many parents respond by tightening control; others back away entirely, hoping peace will return on its own.

Healthy boundaries aren't about control — they're about safety, dignity, and clarity. They say, *"I will stay connected to you while keeping both of us safe."*

Why Boundaries Matter

Boundaries are not barriers; they are bridges built from clarity. They define where one person ends and another begins — the invisible lines that protect both connection and individuality. In healthy families, these lines flex and breathe. But in families facing substance use or mental health struggles, those boundaries blur quickly. Fear and love start to intertwine, and before long, a parent's entire world can collapse around the crisis. It often begins with small, protective instincts: checking a phone, staying up until your teen gets home, scanning for signs of relapse, rehearsing conversations in your head. You start anticipating your loved one's moods before they even speak. You monitor, manage, and absorb their chaos in the name of love. Gradually, your own sleep, work, relationships, and sense of self start to revolve around their well-being.

This happens not because parents are controlling, but often because they are terrified. When someone you love is in danger, hypervigilance feels like devotion. You believe that if you can just pay close enough attention, you can prevent catastrophe. But over time, this vigilance takes a toll. You wake up at every creak in the hallway. You scroll through their social media for clues. Your nervous system stays on high alert long after the immediate crisis has passed. The result is exhaustion — and eventually, resentment — on both sides. The parent becomes depleted, anxious, and increasingly reactive. The young person, meanwhile, feels suffocated and mistrusted. Paradoxically, the more a parent tries to control, the less control they actually have. When one person becomes hyper-responsible, the other often becomes less so. The emotional weight shifts out of balance.

This is where boundaries come in. Boundaries are not punishments or walls; they are guidelines for healthy functioning. They restore equilibrium by giving each person their own work to do. The parent's job is to guide, protect, and provide structure. The adolescent's or young adult's job is to make choices, experience consequences, and learn from them. When those roles get confused — when the parent begins doing the emotional or logistical work of the loved one — growth stalls on both sides. Setting boundaries does not mean caring less. It means caring wisely. It means saying, *"I love you, and I trust that you are capable of learning from your own experiences. I will not carry what is yours to carry."* That's not indifference — that's faith in your loved one's capacity to grow.

Boundaries also communicate respect: *"I trust you to manage your choices, and I will manage mine."* This mutual respect is especially critical in the context of recovery. Substance use and mental health challenges often thrive in environments of chaos, secrecy, and enmeshment — where everyone's emotions become tangled and roles blur. Boundaries restore dignity to both parties. They acknowledge that you are separate people with separate responsibilities, even as you remain connected through care.

One of the hardest truths for parents to accept is that love without limits can become unsustainable. When love morphs into surveillance or sacrifice, it loses its healing power. A parent who never rests, never disconnects, and never says no is not modeling strength — they're modeling burnout. And burnout does not help anyone. Boundaries are how you stay well enough to be effective. They preserve your energy for the moments that matter most. They allow you to offer calm guidance instead of reactive control. They keep your empathy intact, so it does not calcify into resentment.

It is also important to remember that boundaries benefit the young person too. When parents rescue or overfunction, they unintentionally send the message: *"I don't believe you can handle this."* When parents set limits — and hold them with love — they communicate the opposite: *"I believe you are capable of navigating your life, and I trust that struggle is part of learning."* That trust builds internal strength far more effectively than protection ever could. For example, imagine your teen comes home late, violating curfew for the third time. Without boundaries, you might lecture, monitor, or issue an emotional ultimatum — "You're breaking my heart; you never learn." With boundaries, you might calmly say, *"I understand that you want freedom, but being home on time is part of the trust we build. If that can't happen, the consequence is losing access to the car this weekend."* The boundary is clear, the tone is steady, and the responsibility is shared.

Over time, these small moments of boundary-setting accumulate into a new family rhythm — Boundaries are experienced in expectations that are predictable, consequences that are consistent, and emotions that are less explosive. The home begins to feel safer, not because everything is perfect, but because everyone knows where they stand.

Boundaries also protect the relationship itself. Without them, even the deepest love can erode under the weight of unspoken resentment. When parents overextend — emotionally, financially, or logistically — they often reach a breaking point. Anger erupts not because they stopped caring, but because they cared without rest. Setting limits early prevents that buildup. It allows love to remain love, rather than turning into bitterness.

The most effective boundaries are calm, consistent, and compassionate. They don't need to be loud or dramatic. You don't have to justify them endlessly or deliver them as ultimatums. Boundaries gain strength through follow-through, not force. When you hold a limit quietly and reliably, your loved one learns that your words have meaning — and that structure, not chaos, defines the relationship. And remember: boundaries are dynamic. They change as recovery unfolds. What's appropriate at sixteen will differ at twenty-one. Early on, you may need firmer guardrails for safety; later, those can relax to allow independence. The goal is not control, but balance — the flexible give-and-take that allows both parent and loved one to grow.

When families begin to reestablish boundaries, they often notice something surprising: peace. The energy that once went into monitoring and rescuing begins to return. Parents rediscover their own lives — friendships, rest, joy, purpose. That renewed stability becomes part of the healing process. A calm parent provides a regulated nervous system that the young person can eventually borrow from.

Boundaries, then, are not just behavioral; they are emotional and spiritual. They say: *"I am here, but I am also whole."* They remind both parent and loved one that love can coexist with limits, and that autonomy is not abandonment.

In the end, boundaries are the architecture of trust. They give shape to love in families that have been stretched thin by fear. They define a new kind of closeness — one rooted in mutual respect, personal responsibility, and the steady reminder that healing does not mean merging into one another's pain.

It means standing side by side — connected, compassionate, and free.

Punishment vs. Protection

Parents often ask, *"How do I set limits without being harsh?"* It is a good question — and one that gets to the heart of what it means to love someone who is struggling. When fear, exhaustion, and heartbreak mix together, boundaries can easily turn into punishments. But there's a critical difference between the two.

Punishment comes from fear and aims to control. Its unspoken message is, *"If you hurt me, I'll hurt you back."* Protection comes from care and aims to preserve safety. Its message is, *"I won't participate in what hurts either of us."* The difference might sound subtle, but in practice it changes everything — not just for your loved one, but for you.

When a parent sets a punitive boundary, the energy in the room tightens. Voices rise, threats appear, shame fills the air. The focus shifts to the young person's failure, as if fear itself could motivate change. But fear only teaches avoidance. It might produce short-term compliance, but it does not create internal accountability. The loved one may retreat, rebel, or perform good behavior temporarily, but underneath, resentment grows.

Protective boundaries, by contrast, are rooted in respect and love — not emotion in the moment, but a steady commitment to safety for both sides. A protective stance sounds calm, direct, and anchored: *"I love you too much to pretend this is okay."* The goal is not to control the other person's choices, but to define your own participation.

Punishment says, *"I'm reacting to what you did."* Protection says, *"I'm responsible for how I respond."*

Let's look at the contrast:

Punitive Response	Protective Boundary
"You're grounded for a month."	"I'm not comfortable loaning the car until I know you're safe to drive."
"Get out if you use again."	"If you use again tonight, you'll need to stay elsewhere until we can talk with support."
"I'm done with you."	"I love you and can't be around you when you're under the influence."

The language of protection feels different — slower, calmer, less absolute. The difference isn't only in the words; it is in the *tone.* Punishment focuses on failure and control. Protection focuses on shared safety.

Punitive responses often come from a place of panic. A parent sees danger, feels helpless, and instinctively tries to assert control. It is an understandable reflex — the human nervous system equates control with safety. But when fear drives communication, it disconnects rather than corrects. The young person hears the anger but misses the care underneath.

Protective boundaries, on the other hand, come from regulation. They require you to pause before responding, to ground yourself in compassion before speaking. That pause transforms the conversation from reactive to intentional. It tells your loved one, *"I can stay steady even when things are hard."* And that steadiness, more than any rule, teaches accountability.

You can think of the difference this way:

Punishment is about dominance. It says, *"You must feel pain so you'll stop doing this."*

Protection is about safety. It says, *"I'm setting a limit because I care about our wellbeing."*

In recovery work, protection nurtures growth; punishment fuels shame. And shame is one of the most powerful triggers for relapse, secrecy, and emotional withdrawal. Young people who feel shamed tend to hide their struggles rather than seek help for them. But when boundaries are communicated with calm consistency — without judgment — they model how to take responsibility without losing dignity.

Protective boundaries also clarify roles. They remind parents and loved ones alike that each person has agency and choice. A parent can't force sobriety, honesty, or motivation — but they can choose how to engage. They can decide what they will and will not enable, what they will and will not tolerate in their home, and how they will care for themselves in the process.

A helpful mantra is: "I can't control your choices, but I can control my participation."

For example:

Instead of *"If you use again, you're grounded,"* try *"If you use again, I'll need to pause privileges like driving or overnight guests until we can revisit safety."*

Instead of *"You lied to me again — I can't trust you anymore,"* try *"When you lie, it makes it hard to know how to support you. Honesty is what helps us rebuild trust."*

Each protective response holds accountability but preserves connection. It keeps the bridge intact, even when boundaries are firm.

It is important to understand that protective boundaries are not permissive. They are not "soft" or "lenient." In fact, they are often harder to hold because they require emotional regulation. It is easier to shout in anger than to stay calm and clear in love. But the long-term effect is radically different: fear enforces compliance; respect invites cooperation. When parents adopt a protective mindset, they model self-respect. They show their loved one what healthy emotional boundaries look like. Over time, this becomes a template for the young person's own recovery — learning that saying *no* can coexist with care, and that safety does not require control.

In family therapy, we often practice this distinction through role play. Parents learn to speak limits in a grounded tone, using fewer words and more intention. Instead of long lectures or emotional pleas, they practice brief, clear statements anchored in love. The power of protection lies in calm follow-through, not volume.

Consider how each of these examples *feels*:

Punitive: *"You clearly don't care about anyone but your-self."*

Protective: *"I can see you're struggling, and I can't keep arguing like this. I'm going to step away until we can both calm down."*

Punitive: *"You've ruined everything again."*

Protective: *"This hurts to see, and I love you too much to pretend it is okay."*

Notice that the protective version stays rooted in *I* statements — ownership of your feelings and limits — rather than accusations. It de-escalates rather than provokes.

Protection is also reciprocal. It does not just protect the parent's boundaries; it protects the loved one's dignity. It communicates, *"You are still worthy of love, even when your behavior needs to change."* For many young people in recovery, that message is transformative.

To hold this stance consistently, it helps to ground yourself before conversations:

Ask, *"Am I speaking from fear or from care?"*
Breathe before responding.
Remember: the tone you use will teach more than the rule you set.

In the long arc of healing, protection becomes a practice of faith. You're trusting that safety and love can co-exist. You're trusting that limits held with respect will do more to promote accountability than punishment ever could. You're also protecting your own heart. Punishment keeps you locked in cycles of anger and regret. Protection keeps you aligned with your values. It allows you to enforce structure without losing compassion — to say *no* while staying in a relationship.

The shift from punishment to protection may feel awkward at first. You might stumble over your words, or your teen may test your resolve. That's okay. Every time you choose calm over control, you're teaching a new emotional language. Over time, that language becomes the norm.

Because in the end, the goal of parenting through crisis is not to win battles — it is to preserve connection while rebuilding safety. And that's exactly what protection does.

It holds firm where punishment fractures.
It steadies where fear destabilizes.
It loves with limits, not conditions.

And in families facing the storm of substance use or mental health challenges, that difference can mean everything.

How to Set Boundaries That Work

Setting boundaries is not about control — it is about clarity. In families navigating substance use or mental health challenges, clarity becomes a lifeline. When fear rises, everyone's nervous system starts to react instead of responding. Parents over function, young people under function, and chaos fills the space where structure should be. Boundaries bring that structure back.

But not all boundaries work. Some collapse under emotion; others become rigid and punitive. The boundaries that foster healing share a few key qualities: clarity, consistency, calm tone, resilience under pressure, and compassion.

Here's what that looks like in practice.

1. Be Clear and Specific

Ambiguity invites debate. The clearer the boundary, the fewer opportunities for argument or manipulation. When limits are vague, your loved one will test where the edges are — not because they're bad or defiant, but because unclear boundaries create uncertainty. And in families under stress, uncertainty always turns into conflict.

A clear boundary states exactly what you will do and why. It is not about controlling someone else's behavior; it is about defining your own. For example:

"I won't give money for gas if I believe it is being used for substances."

"If you miss curfew again, we'll need to revisit your driving privileges."

"If you're under the influence, I'll need to step away from the conversation until we can talk safely."

Each of these statements does three things: it communicates expectation, it defines consequence, and it centers responsibility on the parent's action, not the loved one's behavior.

The why matters just as much as the what. When you explain your boundary in terms of care — *"because I want us both to be safe,"* or *"because I need to take care of my own wellbeing so I can show up for you"* — it softens the message without diluting it. Boundaries grounded in love are harder to resent, even when they're firm.

2. Stay Consistent

A boundary that changes daily is not a boundary; it is a negotiation. Inconsistency teaches your loved one that persistence, manipulation, or emotional escalation can move the line. Once that happens, the boundary loses its credibility.

Consistency does not mean rigidity — it means reliability. When limits are predictable, your loved one's nervous system begins to feel safer, even if they don't like the rule. Chaos breeds anxiety; predictability builds trust.

If you say, *"I'll pick you up at 10 p.m., and if you're not ready, I'll leave,"* and then you stay until midnight, the message becomes: *"My words don't have weight."* Over time, this erodes respect and increases power struggles. But when you calmly follow through — even once — it reestablishes balance. Your loved one learns, *"They mean what they say, and they're not doing it to punish me."*

Consistency also protects you. When boundaries are clear and stable, you don't have to keep re-calculating where you stand. You save emotional energy for empathy instead of debate.

3. Keep Emotion Low and Language Steady

In boundary-setting, tone is everything. A limit delivered through anger feels like punishment; the same limit delivered calmly feels like protection. When emotions are high, your words lose precision and your message becomes noise.

Say less, mean more. Use short, steady sentences. Avoid long explanations, rationalizations, or lectures — they invite argument and dilute authority. A grounded tone communicates confidence and safety.

For example:

Instead of: "You keep doing this! I've told you so many times, and I'm sick of it!"

Try: "I'm not willing to argue about this again tonight. We'll revisit it when we're calm."

You can even practice your delivery beforehand. Write your boundary out. Read it aloud in a neutral voice. Notice how it feels in your body. If you feel heat in your chest or tightness in your throat, pause until you can speak from steadiness rather than fear.

Tone regulates the nervous system. When your loved one hears calm authority instead of anger, their defenses lower. The message that comes through isn't *"You're in trouble,"* but *"We're safe, and this is the structure we need right now."*

4. Expect Pushback

Many parents are caught off guard when boundaries trigger strong reactions — yelling, crying, guilt, or manipulation. But resistance is not failure. it is proof that the boundary is working. It means you've changed the dance steps, and your loved one is recalibrating.

When you've long operated in a system of over functioning or emotional volatility, a new limit can feel threatening. Your teen or young adult might interpret your steadiness as rejection or control. Stay calm. Reassure them. Reiterate the limit without escalation.

For example:

"I know this feels unfair. You don't have to agree, but this is what I need to feel comfortable."

or

"I can see you're upset. I still love you, and the boundary stands."

The more you hold your ground calmly, the faster the resistance subsides. The moment you react — argue, justify, or overexplain — the focus shifts from the boundary to the power struggle. You lose your anchor.

Think of pushback as part of the learning curve. it is not a reason to backtrack — it is a reminder that change takes repetition.

5. Hold Compassion Alongside Consequence

The most powerful boundaries are not enforced through fear but reinforced through care. When you combine structure with warmth, you teach your loved one that accountability and love can coexist.

After enforcing a boundary, follow tough moments with reassurance. Simple phrases like:

"I still love you. This does not change that."
"I know this is hard. We'll get through it."
"My love isn't conditional on your choices, but my participation is."

These small statements carry enormous emotional weight. They soften defensiveness, counter shame, and keep the relationship intact. They say, *"Even when there are consequences, you're not alone."*

Boundaries without compassion feel cold; compassion without boundaries feels chaotic. Healing requires both.

Boundaries in Practice

Here's how this might look in real life:

Scenario: Your young adult has been using substances and borrowing your car. You're terrified they'll get into an accident.

Without Boundaries: You lecture them, demand they stop, threaten to take the keys, but later give in when they promise to "do better."

Punitive Boundary: *"You're irresponsible! I'm taking the car forever."*

Protective Boundary: *"I love you, and I can't lend the car right now. When you've had a period of stability and we can both feel confident about safety, we'll revisit it."*

Notice the difference in tone. The first escalates; the second contains.

Boundaries that work are not about winning arguments — they're about creating safety and predictability. They reduce chaos by defining reality. They teach both parent and loved one how to stay connected *without* losing individuality.

When Boundaries Fail — and How to Recover

Even the strongest boundaries will get tested. You'll lose your cool, overreact, or backtrack at times. That's normal. The key is repair. When you notice yourself slipping, name it without shame:

"I overreacted earlier. I still stand by the boundary, but I wish I'd said it more calmly."

Repair models self-awareness. It teaches your loved one that limits don't require perfection — just honesty.

Consistency will always matter more than control. Each time you follow through calmly, you strengthen both trust and respect. Over time, those two ingredients become the real boundary — the invisible framework that holds the family steady through recovery. Boundaries that work are living things. They breathe, adapt, and grow as your family does. They are the steady rhythm beneath the storm — not harsh, not rigid, but reliably there. When you hold them with love and consistency, you communicate the most healing message possible:

"I love you enough to stay connected, and I love you enough to stay whole."

That balance — between empathy and structure, between heart and backbone — is where real change begins.

When Boundaries Feel Cruel

For many parents, boundaries are not the hard part — holding them is. The most painful moments often arrive *after* you've set a limit. When you follow through on a boundary and watch your loved one struggle, cry, or lash out, every instinct in you screams to reverse it. The emotional pull to protect them can feel overwhelming. It is the ache of love colliding with reality.

Many parents describe this experience as heartbreaking — not because they doubt the boundary's importance, but because it goes against every fiber of what it means to be a caregiver. You've spent years smoothing paths, catching falls, and minimizing pain. Suddenly you're being asked to do the opposite: to stand back and let natural consequences unfold. To watch someone you love suffer, and *not* intervene, feels like cruelty. And yet, shielding them from pain often prolongs it. When parents step in too soon, they interrupt the very learning process that could help their loved one grow. Pain — in the right dose, with the right support — is not the enemy. It is information. It teaches cause and effect, responsibility, and resilience.

Boundaries, in this sense, become acts of faith. They ask you to believe that growth is possible even through discomfort. They require you to trust that your loved one's capacity for adaptation is greater than their fear — and sometimes greater than your own. It is the difference between abandonment and accountability. Abandonment says, *"You're on your own."* Accountability says, *"I love you enough to let reality do some of the teaching."* Letting your loved one experience the consequences of their actions is not cruelty; it is compassion that has learned restraint. It is love with boundaries around it — love that says, *"I will walk beside you, but I won't carry what isn't mine."*

A parent once told me, *"Every time I rescued him, I robbed him of the chance to rescue himself."* That moment of awareness transformed her parenting. She stopped seeing herself as her son's savior and began seeing herself as his steady witness — the calm presence who believed in his capacity to rise. It wasn't easy. There were nights of silence, tears, and doubt. But over time, she began to see small changes — her son taking responsibility, making choices, learning from mistakes. He started building muscles she had unknowingly been using for him.

Boundaries feel cruel because love without rescue feels unnatural. But over time, many parents discover something surprising: when they stop rescuing, the relationship deepens. Without the constant dance of control and dependence, authenticity reemerges. Conversations shift from "fixing" to "witnessing." The parent becomes not a manager of behavior but a model of stability.

The paradox of parenting through crisis is that sometimes the most loving action is restraint. You are not withholding care — you are redefining it. Instead of intervening in every crisis, you're saying, *"I believe you are capable of learning from this."* Instead of softening every consequence, you're saying, *"I trust that discomfort won't destroy you."* This does not mean stepping away entirely. Boundaries are not about emotional withdrawal. They're about staying present — remaining available, calm, and loving while allowing your loved one to meet their own reality. The line is fine but profound: it is the shift from *"I'll fix this for you"* to *"I'll stand beside you while you figure it out."*

Here's how that might look in practice:

When your teen fails a class:

Instead of rushing to email the teacher or arrange tutoring that same night, you might say, *"That must feel discouraging. Let's talk about what support you want moving forward."* You're not rescuing; you're inviting reflection.

When your young adult loses a job:

Instead of immediately offering money or solutions, you might say, *"I know that's hard. I trust you'll find your footing. How can I support you in brainstorming next steps?"* You're offering partnership, not pity.

When substance use causes chaos:

Instead of hiding the problem or cleaning up the mess, you might say, *"I love you deeply, and I can't participate in anything that puts either of us at risk. When you're ready to make a change, I'll help you find the right support."* You're expressing love through clarity, not control.

Every one of these responses honors the same principle: *Love can coexist with boundaries.*

Still, it is important to acknowledge that the emotional toll of boundary-setting is real. Parents in this position often describe living in a constant state of internal tension — a mix of guilt, fear, and second-guessing. You may lie awake at night wondering if you've done the right thing, if you were too harsh, if your loved one now feels unloved. This inner conflict is normal. it is a sign that you care deeply and that you're trying to love in a new way — one that balances empathy with accountability.

If you notice yourself struggling to tolerate the discomfort of your loved one's pain, try grounding in self-compassion. Remind yourself: *"I am not being cruel. I am honoring the process that allows both of us to heal."*

You can even say this silently when guilt rises:

"I can love them and still let them learn."
"Their struggle does not mean I failed."
"Boundaries are not rejection; they're protection."

Sometimes, it helps to remember what would happen without the boundary. Without limits, crises repeat. Resentment grows. The home becomes unpredictable, and trust erodes on both sides. Holding the boundary, however painful, interrupts that cycle. It creates a moment of pause where something new can begin.

In the language of family systems, boundaries introduce friction — but friction is often the first step toward balance. The system can't stabilize until patterns change, and patterns can't change without discomfort. That discomfort, as painful as it is, signals movement.

You are not being cruel for allowing your loved one to face consequences. You are inviting growth that can only happen through experience. In doing so, you're also protecting your own wellbeing — and modeling for your loved one what self-respect looks like.

Boundaries are acts of faith, but they are also acts of endurance. They require patience to withstand the in-between — the space between setting the limit and seeing the outcome. That space can feel unbearable at times. It helps to remember that healing rarely happens on your timeline. It unfolds on its own, often in the quiet moments after the boundary has been held.

Sometimes, your loved one will respond with anger or distance. They may accuse you of not caring, or of giving up on them. It will sting. But your calm consistency will speak louder than your words. Over time, they begin to feel what they couldn't yet hear — that your restraint was never abandonment; it was love in its most mature form.

There is an old saying in recovery circles: *"You can't do someone else's growing for them."* Boundaries honor that truth. They make space for personal responsibility and the dignity that comes with it. When parents rescue too quickly, they unintentionally interrupt their loved one's chance to develop self-efficacy — the belief that they can survive difficulty and make change.

By holding the boundary, you are helping them build that belief. You are showing them, even in silence, *"I have faith in you."*

Boundaries may feel cruel in the moment, but over time, they reveal themselves as one of the purest expressions of love — love that trusts the process, love that stays steady when everything else wavers, love that allows growth to happen even when it hurts. Because the goal isn't to spare your loved one from every consequence. It is to help them discover their own strength, while knowing that, through it all, they are still loved — fiercely, steadily, and without condition.

Reflection & Practice

1. Write down one boundary you avoid setting. What fear stops you? Rephrase that boundary as a statement of care instead of control.
2. Identify one area where you overextend yourself. How might stepping back restore balance without withdrawal?
3. Practice saying a boundary aloud in a calm voice. Notice how your body feels. Ground yourself before the conversation.
4. Afterward, acknowledge your effort. Boundaries are not walls; they are bridges with clear entry points.

Chapter 5

The Power of Natural Consequences

Every parent wants to protect their loved one from pain. It is instinctive — the impulse to cushion, fix, explain, and rescue. But when we shield too much, we unintentionally interfere with one of life's greatest teachers: the natural consequence.

Natural consequences aren't punishments. They're the organic results of choices — missed deadlines, strained friendships, lost privileges, or unexpected discomforts that reveal cause and effect. When parents allow natural consequences to unfold in safe and loving contexts, they help their loved one develop responsibility, resilience, and emotional maturity.

The key is staying close enough for safety, but far away enough for growth.

Why Natural Consequences Work

One of the hardest lessons for any parent to accept is that discomfort is often the soil where growth takes root. It can feel unbearable to watch a loved one suffer, to see them stumble or make mistakes that seem preventable. Yet it is precisely in those moments—when choices meet reality—that true learning happens. The human brain is designed to grow through experience, not instruction. It is one thing to hear a rule; it is another to feel its truth. When someone directly experiences the link between behavior and outcome—between choice and consequence—the brain's learning circuits activate, strengthening the neural pathways associated with reflection, accountability, and problem-solving. The lesson becomes embodied, not theoretical. Punishment, by contrast, short-circuits that process. Its goal is often control: to make someone behave differently through fear, shame, or authority. It might produce obedience in the moment, but it rarely produces insight. When a young person is punished harshly, their brain shifts into survival mode. The amygdala, the brain's alarm system, floods the body with stress signals, narrowing focus to self-protection rather than understanding. The message received is not *"I need to think about my choices"* but *"I need to avoid getting caught."* Punishment teaches avoidance; natural consequences teach reflection.

This distinction matters profoundly in families coping with substance use or mental-health challenges. When a parent imposes constant rules, lectures, and punishments, the dynamic often turns into a power struggle. The loved one resists control, and the parent doubles down, creating a cycle of fear and defiance. Natural consequences break that cycle by transferring responsibility back to where it belongs. Instead of saying, *"You'll obey because I said so,"* a parent communicates, *"Life has its own feedback, and I trust you can learn from it."* This shift reframes the relationship: the parent becomes a guide rather than an enforcer, and the loved one begins to see themselves not as a problem to be managed but as a person capable of growth.

Natural consequences also preserve dignity. When a young person experiences the results of their choices—missing an important event because they overslept, losing trust after lying, or feeling the emotional fallout of substance use—they are not being shamed; they are being invited into accountability. They remain the central actor in their own story, rather than a passive recipient of punishment. The emotional tone changes from *"You failed me"* to *"You're capable of learning."* That subtle shift nurtures self-respect, which is essential for recovery and long-term maturity.

From a neuroscience perspective, this process makes sense. Adolescents and young adults are still developing the prefrontal cortex—the part of the brain responsible for impulse control, decision-making, and understanding long-term consequences. Experience, not lecture, is what strengthens that region. Each time a young person encounters a natural consequence and reflects on it, the brain's frontal networks gain resilience. This is how accountability becomes internalized. Words alone cannot accomplish what experience can.

For parents, however, allowing natural consequences can feel almost impossible. It requires letting go of control and tolerating uncertainty. Many parents worry that standing back will appear cold or uncaring. Yet the opposite is true. Allowing a loved one to experience reality is one of the most compassionate acts a parent can offer. It communicates, *"I believe in your ability to face this and to learn from it."* Stepping back does not mean stepping away; it means shifting from rescue to support, from control to containment. The parent remains a safe base, a steady witness, and an emotional anchor while life delivers the lesson. This can sound abstract until it is lived. Imagine your teenager stays up all night gaming and oversleeps, missing an exam. The natural consequence is the disappointment and potential academic setback that follows. The parent who calls the teacher to smooth things over might feel helpful in the moment but unintentionally robs the loved one of learning cause and effect. Or picture a young adult who spends their paycheck recklessly and cannot afford their share of rent. Bailing them out immediately may soothe short-term distress but undermines long-term responsibility. In each of these moments, discomfort—not rescue—creates growth.

Allowing these lessons to unfold does not mean withholding empathy. It means pairing structure with compassion. You can say, *"I know this feels awful, and I trust you'll find a way through it."* That combination—acknowledgment plus confidence—helps your loved one integrate both emotion and accountability. Your calm presence signals that mistakes are survivable and that learning can happen without shame.

Of course, natural consequences have limits. They work best when safety is not at immediate risk. In cases involving active substance use, suicidal behavior, or severe mental-health crises, protective boundaries and professional help must take precedence. The goal is never to let someone spiral into danger; it is to allow manageable discomfort within a structure of safety. Balance is key: structure provides containment, while natural consequences provide growth. Together, they cultivate maturity.

Parents often describe the internal battle that comes with this approach. The urge to step in—to rescue, fix, or soften the blow—can be overwhelming. It feels counterintuitive to love someone and not remove their pain. But rescuing too quickly sends a subtle message: *"You can't handle this."* Over time, that message weakens confidence and fuels dependency. Allowing natural consequences, by contrast, communicates faith: *"You are strong enough to face this, and I'm here while you do."* That faith becomes the foundation for resilience. When families begin to practice this shift, the household energy often changes. There is less yelling, less chasing, fewer negotiations. Parents stop hovering and start observing. Young people, no longer trapped in a cycle of control and rebellion, begin to feel ownership of their choices. Even setbacks start to look different—they become opportunities to reflect rather than reasons to fight. The entire family system breathes a little easier.

Over time, the results of this approach are subtle but profound. Parents find that their loved ones start taking initiative: calling a teacher on their own, managing money more thoughtfully, seeking help after a mistake. The parent's role evolves from crisis manager to mentor. What emerges is a quieter kind of authority—one grounded in steadiness rather than power. Natural consequences work because they align with how both the brain and the heart grow. They teach not through fear, but through experience. They invite ownership instead of resistance. They replace control with trust. And most of all, they honor the dignity of both parent and loved one.

So when you find yourself standing in that painful space—watching your loved one face the results of their choices and wanting desperately to step in—pause. Breathe. Remember that stepping back is not abandonment; it is belief. You are saying, *"I trust that you can learn from this. I believe in your ability to change."* That belief, steady and loving, is what makes growth possible.

In the end, natural consequences do more than correct behavior—they cultivate wisdom. They teach that actions matter, that recovery is built on ownership, and that love can coexist with limits. They allow both parent and loved one to grow side by side, each learning the same essential truth: that healing happens not through control, but through courage, compassion, and the willingness to let life be the teacher.

When to Step In

The philosophy of natural consequences rests on a delicate balance between trust and protection. Allowing a loved one to experience the results of their choices is one of the most powerful teachers in life — but not every outcome should be allowed to unfold. Some consequences cross a line from discomfort into danger, from growth into potential trauma. The art of parenting through substance use and mental-health challenges lies in learning to discern the difference.

The central question is not *"Should I intervene?"* but *"What kind of discomfort am I allowing, and what kind of danger am I preventing?"* The goal is not to shield your loved one from every struggle — struggle is part of learning — but to step in when the stakes become unsafe, unmanageable, or developmentally beyond their capacity to handle.

You can start by asking yourself three simple but profound questions:

Is this consequence painful or is it harmful?

Painful experiences are those that sting but don't endanger — the kinds of lessons that can be metabolized into insight. Missing a deadline, failing a test, losing a friendship, or facing the disappointment of a broken trust — these are painful, but they're survivable. They teach cause and effect without threatening safety. Harmful consequences, on the other hand, carry the potential for irreversible damage. Driving while impaired, experimenting with unknown substances, being in unsafe environments, or engaging in self-destructive behavior, are not learning opportunities; they are emergencies. In those moments, stepping in isn't interference — it is protection. The role of a parent is not to eliminate all pain, but to be alert to preventable harm.

Can the situation be repaired?

A useful lens for deciding when to intervene is to ask whether the consequence can be undone or repaired. Academic or social setbacks often fall into the category of repairable: a failed class can be retaken; a lost privilege can be earned back. These situations invite growth through effort and reflection. But physical injury, sexual exploitation, overdose, or legal crises carry permanent implications. They are not learning experiences; they are critical thresholds where parental action is not only justified but essential. In those moments, love must act swiftly, even if it means temporarily overriding autonomy.

Is the lesson proportional to the behavior?

Proportionality is another key consideration. The goal of natural consequences is to let reality deliver the appropriate feedback — not to let a minor mistake spiral into devastation. Forgetting a homework assignment might result in a lower grade — a natural, proportional outcome that fosters accountability. But ignoring mounting substance use until a young person becomes homeless or seriously ill is not proportional — it is perilous. Parents must constantly weigh the potential impact of inaction against the developmental capacity of their loved one to learn from it. A sixteen-year-old experimenting with marijuana after stress is not the same as a twenty-year-old driving under the influence. Context matters.

Holding this discernment requires self-awareness. Fear can make every situation feel urgent. Parents must learn to anchor themselves in reflection rather than reaction. A calm internal question like, *"Is my loved one uncomfortable, or are they unsafe?"* helps differentiate between moments that require patience and those that require intervention.

The truth is, no parent gets this perfectly right. The line between discomfort and danger is not always clear in real time. It often becomes visible only in hindsight. What matters most is not perfection, but presence — the willingness to keep assessing, adjusting, and learning alongside your loved one.

Parents are not meant to be puppet masters, pulling strings to control every move. They are the safety net — strong, steady, and responsive when a fall becomes too great. A net does not prevent every slip; it catches what would cause irreparable harm. Similarly, boundaries and natural consequences are not about detachment, but about holding that net with awareness. You allow discomfort to teach, but you intervene when the consequence threatens to break something that cannot easily be mended.

In practice, this might look like stepping back when your loved one faces social fallout for breaking a promise but stepping in immediately if you discover they are being coerced or abused. It means allowing them to feel the embarrassment of failing a test but intervening if the failure stems from untreated depression or suicidal thinking. It means tolerating the ache of watching them struggle with peers but seeking help when isolation turns into despair. This discernment becomes a daily practice — one that refines over time. Parents who learn to differentiate between discomfort and danger begin to feel less reactive and more grounded. They can allow appropriate struggle without collapsing into guilt or panic. Their loved ones, in turn, begin to feel both freer and safer — freer to make mistakes, safer to know that when things truly become overwhelming, help will come.

Knowing when to step in also requires support. Parents are not meant to hold these decisions alone. Consulting with a family therapist, addiction specialist, or adolescent mental-health professional can provide an objective lens when emotions cloud judgment. Professionals can help you build what clinicians call a "graduated response plan" — a framework that outlines which situations warrant stepping back and which require stepping in.

Ultimately, stepping in at the right moments does not undermine independence — it preserves it. It ensures that learning happens within a structure of safety rather than chaos. It communicates: *"I will let you face what you can handle, and I will protect you from what you cannot."* That balance — between protection and trust — is the heart of effective parenting through crisis. It is what allows you to be both a safety net and a springboard, guiding your loved one toward responsibility without abandoning them to danger.

So when you find yourself questioning whether to intervene, pause and breathe. Ask: *Is this pain constructive or destructive? Is this a lesson, or a risk? Is this discomfort leading toward growth, or toward harm?* The answers may not always be immediate, but your attunement — your willingness to ask these questions — is itself a form of love.

Parenting through uncertainty is never clean or simple. But with each decision, each moment of reflection, you are strengthening the most important bond of all: the trust that says, *"I will not rescue you from every fall, but I will provide a net when the is from too great a height."*

The Balance Between Support and Rescue

Letting a young person experience the consequences of their actions is not an act of neglect — it is an act of faith. It says, *"I believe in your ability to learn, adapt, and grow."* Yet this belief is one of the hardest things for a parent to hold, especially when the stakes feel so high. The tension between support and rescue lives at the core of parenting through crisis. It is where love meets anxiety, where care risks turning into control. The instinct to rescue is primal. When you see your loved one suffering, your whole body responds — heart racing, stomach tight, mind searching for solutions. Every impulse says, *Fix it. Make it stop.* You remember the years when protecting them from pain was not only possible but necessary: when you held their hand across the street, zipped their coat, or wiped their tears after a fall. But adolescence and young adulthood bring a new kind of fall — one that no parent can prevent, only accompany. The hardest lesson for loving parents to learn is that sometimes helping can hurt.

Many parents intervene not because they doubt their loved one's resilience, but because their own anxiety becomes unbearable. Watching a loved one struggle feels intolerable, so they step in to relieve that discomfort — both theirs and their loved one's. The problem is that emotional rescue, though well-intentioned, often prevents growth. The immediate relief of fixing a problem can create long-term dependence. When a parent repeatedly shields a young person from the natural consequences of their choices, they send an unintended message: *"You can't handle this; I must handle it for you."* Over time, that message erodes confidence and reinforces helplessness. Rescue is seductive because it feels compassionate. But compassion without boundaries quickly turns into management. The difference lies in who holds the responsibility for change. Rescue takes the burden away from the person who needs to learn; support stands beside them as they carry it.

Therapists often describe the alternative to rescue as the coaching stance — an approach that is supportive, steady, and curious, but not overinvolved. A coach does not play the game for the athlete; they observe, guide, and provide structure for growth. They let the player make mistakes because mistakes are how skills develop. Likewise, the coaching stance invites parents to stay present and engaged without taking over. It says, *"I'm with you, not in front of you."*

In practical terms, this might look like sitting beside your loved one while they make a difficult phone call to a teacher or counselor — but not making the call for them. It might mean driving them to a therapy appointment after they have broken curfew or violated a boundary — but letting them do the talking once they arrive. It might mean helping them plan a strategy to repay borrowed money after impulsive spending — but resisting the urge to replace it for them.

In each example, the parent provides structure and presence, but not rescue. The message is consistent: *"You're not alone, but this is your work."*

Presence matters more than solutions. When a young person knows that a parent is near — calm, compassionate, and confident in their capacity — they begin to internalize that same confidence. They learn that accountability and love can coexist, that consequences are not the opposite of care, and that failure is not fatal. This kind of support fosters what psychologists call earned efficacy — the lived experience of realizing, *"I can do hard things, and the people who love me believe that too."*

There's another subtle but vital piece to this balance: timing. True support often requires pausing before acting. Parents who can tolerate their own anxiety long enough to let their loved one try — and maybe fail — create space for resilience to form. That pause can feel endless in the moment, but it is where growth happens. Each time a parent waits, resists the urge to rescue, and instead says, *"What's your plan?"* or *"How do you want to handle this?"* they transfer ownership back where it belongs.

This does not mean withdrawing care. In fact, maintaining emotional availability is what allows natural consequences to be tolerable. The coaching stance is both warm and boundaried — it holds space without absorbing the problem. Parents often fear that this detachment will make them seem cold or indifferent. But the opposite is true. When you are grounded and clear, your presence becomes a stabilizing force. You model what emotional regulation looks like under stress.

Sometimes, the balance between support and rescue becomes visible only in hindsight. A parent who often jumped in to negotiate with school administrators or employers may later realize that doing so prevented their loved one from developing advocacy skills. A parent who paid off a substance-related debt might later see that, while it avoided an immediate crisis, it also delayed accountability. Recognizing these patterns is not about blame — it is about awareness. You can always adjust, always recalibrate, always begin again.

Finding this balance also means recognizing your own triggers. Ask yourself: *When do I feel most compelled to rescue?* Often, it is when you're anxious, guilty, or afraid of judgment. Those emotions are powerful drivers, but they are not reliable guides. Before stepping in, it can help to pause and ask:

Is this about my loved one's safety or my own discomfort?
Am I preventing harm or preventing growth?
What lesson might they miss if I solve this for them?

These questions help shift the focus from reaction to reflection. They slow down the automatic rescue reflex and allow more intentional choices.

In families navigating substance use or mental-health issues, the line between support and rescue can blur easily. The stakes are high, and fear can masquerade as love. But love that rescues every time eventually collapses under its own weight. Sustainable love — the kind that fosters healing — holds steady even when it hurts. It trusts the process, even when outcomes are uncertain.

A parent reported the following anecdote which illustrates the shift that is possible. Her young adult son, recently in early recovery, had lost his job after missing several shifts. Her first instinct was to call his employer and plead for a second chance. Instead, she took a breath and waited. Later, she told me, *"He was furious at first, but a week later, he applied somewhere else — on his own. He got the job. I realized he didn't need me to save him. He needed me to believe he could save himself."* That story captures the essence of balance: stepping back without stepping away. When parents find the courage to hold that space, they give their loved one the chance to meet themselves — to experience both consequence and capability.

Ultimately, support without rescue says, *"I love you enough to let you grow."* It replaces panic with patience, control with compassion, and fear with faith. It allows both parent and loved one to share the same truth — that love is not about doing everything for each other, but about believing in each other's capacity to do what's necessary.

In the long arc of recovery and maturation, this kind of faith becomes the path between dependence and independence, between crisis and stability, between who a young person has been and who they are becoming. It is not an easy journey, but it is the one that allows love to mature alongside them — steady, clear, and enduring.

The Neuroscience of Learning

At its core, the process of learning — whether in therapy, recovery, or everyday life — is biological. It is not only about insight or willpower but about how the brain encodes experience. Every time we make a choice and observe its result, the brain updates its understanding of cause and effect. This feedback loop — *I act, something happens, I reflect, I adjust* — is the same neurological process that cognitive-behavioral therapy relies on. It is also the foundation of how accountability, emotional regulation, and wisdom take shape.

Natural consequences engage these learning circuits in a way that words alone cannot. When a young person experiences the direct result of their actions — being late and missing an opportunity, lying and feeling the sting of broken trust, spending recklessly and facing financial strain — the brain registers that experience as data. The anterior cingulate cortex, which monitors error detection and emotional awareness, lights up. The prefrontal cortex, responsible for planning and decision-making, begins to integrate that data into future behavior. Through repetition, these neural pathways strengthen, helping the brain associate specific actions with specific outcomes. When parents remove every obstacle or prevent discomfort, they interrupt this essential loop. The brain isn't allowed the opportunity to connect behavior with effect, so the circuitry for accountability does not develop. Without that connection, learning remains theoretical — understood in words but not in lived experience. A loved one might intellectually know that lying has consequences, but if those consequences are always softened or erased, the emotional and cognitive integration never occurs. The lesson remains external — "Mom or Dad will fix it" — rather than internal — "My actions have an impact, and I can make different choices next time."

The real power of learning lies in experiencing the full sequence: *I made a choice → I felt the result → I can choose differently next time.* That middle step — *feeling the result* — is where change begins. It is not about punishment or shame; it is about letting the nervous system register feedback. This is how the brain learns self-regulation — through titrated tolerance of discomfort, reflection, and then adjusting behavior accordingly. Teens and young adults who practice this loop early develop what psychologists call internal locus of control — the belief that they can influence outcomes through their own actions. This sense of agency is crucial in recovery from substance use and mental health challenges. It replaces helplessness with empowerment. Instead of thinking, *"Things happen to me,"* the young person begins to think, *"My choices shape what happens next."*

When this process is disrupted — by overprotection, avoidance, or chronic rescuing — the brain does not get to practice resilience. Without repeated exposure to manageable consequences, the neural circuits that govern patience, reflection, and impulse control remain underdeveloped. The young person may grow up emotionally intelligent but practically untested. They may know right from wrong but lack the emotional muscle to navigate discomfort.

Neuroscientifically, this learning process mirrors what therapists cultivate in cognitive-behavioral therapy and other evidence-based treatments. Clients identify patterns of thought and behavior, test them against real-world outcomes, and learn through feedback what works and what does not. Natural consequences are the real-life extension of this same process — the lab of daily living. Each time a young person acts, experiences feedback, and reflects, the neural circuitry for accountability and adaptation strengthens.

Parents often worry that allowing natural consequences will damage their relationship with their loved one or make them seem unsupportive. In truth, it does the opposite when done with empathy. When a parent can stay calm and compassionate — allowing discomfort while staying emotionally present — they send a powerful signal to their loved one's nervous system: *"You are safe enough to learn."* That safety allows the brain to process feedback without shame. The lesson becomes integrated, not internalized as punishment. Over time, these small cycles of learning create lasting change. The young person's brain begins to predict the outcomes of their actions before they occur — a function known as prospective learning. They start to pause, anticipate, and make conscious choices instead of reactive ones. This is the foundation of self-regulation — the ability to tolerate emotion, think clearly under stress, and respond intentionally rather than impulsively.

Self-regulation is the cornerstone of emotional maturity, healthy relationships, and sustained recovery. It is not something that can be taught through lecture or logic alone; it must be practiced, felt, and reinforced through lived experience. Each time a young person encounters a consequence, reflects on it, and chooses differently, their brain is literally rewiring toward resilience.

For parents, understanding this process can help ease the guilt that often accompanies letting a loved one struggle. You are not being cruel by allowing discomfort — you are allowing the brain to do what it was built to do: learn through experience. You are trusting the natural intelligence of the nervous system to adapt, integrate, and grow. In this way, natural consequences are not just behavioral tools; they are neurological allies. They help shape the architecture of accountability, empathy, and foresight. They teach young people that life is not something to fear or control but something to engage with — to learn from, and to grow through.

When parents can stay steady during this process — allowing feedback without panic, providing empathy without interference — they create the ideal learning environment for the developing brain. The message becomes clear: *"You are capable. You can make choices, experience outcomes, and learn from them. I am here while you do."*

That is how self-regulation takes root — not in avoidance of discomfort, but in the confidence that even discomfort can be survived, understood, and transformed. Loved ones who internalize that truth carry it with them into adulthood. It becomes part of their internal blueprint.

Common Pitfalls

Even the most well-intentioned parents can lose their footing when trying to balance support, boundaries, and love. The emotional terrain of parenting through substance use or mental-health challenges is complex; fear and care often blur together. It is easy to slip into patterns that feel helpful in the moment but ultimately undermine growth and connection. These missteps aren't signs of failure — they're signs of being human, of loving deeply and wanting desperately to protect. Recognizing them is the first step toward change.

One of the most common traps is over-rescuing. This happens when parents fix problems not because their loved one truly cannot handle them, but because the parent cannot tolerate watching them struggle. It is the instinct to step in and smooth things over — to email the teacher, replace the lost money, or apologize on behalf of your loved one — all in the name of love. On the surface, these actions seem compassionate. But underneath, they often stem from the parent's own anxiety and discomfort with uncertainty. Over time, these rescues communicate an unintended message: *"You're not capable of handling this on your own."* The result is dependence instead of confidence, learned helplessness instead of resilience.

Over-rescuing is often driven by fear — fear that if a mistake isn't corrected immediately, it will spiral into catastrophe. But when parents take over too quickly, they rob their loved one of the essential link between action and outcome. Without that link, the young person never gets to experience the pride that comes from self-correction or problem-solving. They may begin to rely on others to fix situations, or conversely, to rebel against perceived control. In either case, autonomy is lost.

On the opposite end of the spectrum is over-detaching. This occurs when parents, exhausted or trying to follow advice about "tough love," swing too far in the other direction. They step back completely, withholding empathy in the name of letting their loved one "learn the hard way." While the intention may be to promote independence, the impact can be painful. A young person navigating shame, fear, or mental-health challenges may interpret detachment as rejection. Instead of fostering accountability, it can fuel despair or defiance. Healthy detachment is not emotional withdrawal; it is emotional regulation. It is possible to hold boundaries and still show compassion. When parents disconnect completely — refusing to listen, cutting off communication, or using silence as a teaching tool — they inadvertently reinforce the shame that drives many self-destructive behaviors in the first place. Growth requires safety, and safety requires connection. Without warmth and empathy, consequences lose their power to teach and begin to wound instead.

The third pitfall is moralizing — turning consequences into lectures, sermons, or guilt-laden "teachable moments." Phrases like *"I hope you've learned your lesson,"* or *"You see what happens when you don't listen?"* come from frustration and fear, but they rarely create reflection. Instead, they create shame. And shame is one of the brain's biggest barriers to learning. When a young person feels shamed, their nervous system goes into defense mode. The prefrontal cortex — the part of the brain responsible for reasoning and insight — shuts down. They may appear defiant, but internally they are flooded with emotion, unable to process feedback.

Moralizing also shifts the focus from reflection to performance. The loved one learns how to appear remorseful rather than how to think critically about their choices. They might say what they think the parent wants to hear — *"I know, I messed up, I'll do better"* — but the underlying learning does not integrate. True accountability arises from curiosity and connection, not from shame or lecture.

The antidote to all three of these pitfalls — over-rescuing, over-detaching, and moralizing — is empathy paired with restraint. Empathy without restraint leads to enmeshment; restraint without empathy leads to isolation. But together, they create a balance that fosters growth.

Empathy acknowledges the pain of the moment; restraint allows the consequence to do its work.

In practice, this balance might sound like: *"I know this feels hard. I trust you can handle it, and I'm here if you need support."* This simple statement does several powerful things at once. It validates the emotional experience, communicates faith in the loved one's capacity, and keeps the relationship open. It neither rescues nor abandons. It sits in the middle — what therapists sometimes call *the sweet spot of connection without control.*

When parents find that middle ground, something remarkable happens. The young person begins to internalize two truths at once: *"My feelings are real,"* and *"I am capable of handling them."* That combination builds emotional resilience and self-trust — the twin foundations of recovery and independence.

Avoiding these pitfalls does not mean you'll never overstep or pull back too far. Every parent oscillates between extremes at times. The goal isn't perfect balance but awareness. When you notice yourself rescuing, detaching, or moralizing, you can pause, take a breath, and reorient. You can return to empathy and restraint — to the steady center that says, *"I love you, and I trust you to do your part."*

That stance, more than any lecture or intervention, is what teaches the deepest lesson: that love can be both firm and kind, and that accountability and connection can coexist.

Creating Safe Containers for Consequences

Natural consequences are most effective when they unfold inside a framework of stability and care. Think of yourself not as the architect of the lesson, but as the builder of the *container* in which the lesson takes place. A container provides boundaries — it holds, supports, and protects — without taking over. When a young person knows that consequences will occur within a predictable, emotionally safe environment, their nervous system can tolerate discomfort long enough to learn from it. Without that safety, consequences simply feel like punishment or chaos.

Creating a safe container begins long before a crisis happens. It requires consistency, communication, and calm follow-through. The process isn't about control — it is about creating the conditions in which accountability can take root. Each step of the process — anticipating, communicating, holding steady, and reflecting — plays a crucial role in transforming experience into growth.

1. Anticipate

The first step in creating a safe container is anticipation. This means discussing potential outcomes *before* they happen. These are not warnings or threats; they are collaborative conversations about what choices might lead to. Anticipation turns consequences from surprises into expectations. For example: *"If you don't finish the project, the grade will reflect that. I won't email the teacher for you."* or *"If you use substances, we'll need to take a break from having friends over until things feel stable."*

When expectations are discussed in advance, consequences feel fair and predictable rather than punitive. The brain learns best in predictable environments — uncertainty triggers anxiety and defensiveness, while predictability creates the safety needed for reflection. By anticipating outcomes calmly, you help your loved one's nervous system prepare for accountability instead of resisting it.

2. Communicate

Once expectations are set, the next step is clear and calm communication. Consequences lose their power when they are delivered reactively — in anger, sarcasm, or confusion. Communicating boundaries in a steady tone communicates respect. It says, *"I take you seriously, and I trust you can handle this conversation."* Avoid surprises. Ambiguity breeds resentment and argument. When a young person does not know what to expect, they're more likely to interpret a consequence as punishment rather than as a natural result of their choice. When you're consistent in your communication — *"If this happens, here's how I'll respond"* — your loved one can connect action and outcome without getting lost in emotion. This predictability helps them internalize responsibility instead of reacting against it.

3. Hold Steady

Perhaps the hardest part of this process comes next: holding steady when the consequence arrives. This is the moment when every parental instinct to rescue or soften reemerges. The sight of your loved one in pain — crying, angry, blaming, or ashamed — can feel unbearable. But intervening too soon undoes the learning. It communicates, *"I don't believe you can handle this discomfort,"* even when your words say otherwise.

Holding steady does not mean being silent or cold. It means staying calm, grounded, and compassionate. Quiet empathy is more powerful than rescue. You might say, *"I know this feels hard. I'm here if you want to talk."* You're not fixing, but you're also not abandoning. You're holding space — letting your presence be the container while the lesson unfolds. This step requires self-regulation. If you feel your own anxiety rising, take a breath before responding. Remind yourself that discomfort is not danger. Learning is happening, even if it looks messy. Trust the process: the consequence, not the correction, will do the teaching.

4. Reflect Together

The final — and most transformative — step is reflection. After emotions cool, revisit the experience together. This is where insight forms. Reflection turns experience into growth by connecting feelings, actions, and lessons. The conversation does not need to be long or formal; in fact, shorter is often better. You might simply ask: *"What did you notice?"* or *"What might you do differently next time?"*

Reflection works because it engages the prefrontal cortex — the part of the brain that integrates emotion and reasoning. When your loved one reflects, they're practicing self-awareness, problem-solving, and emotional regulation all at once. You can model this by reflecting aloud yourself: *"I know that was hard for me to watch. I wanted to step in, but I'm glad I let you handle it."* This kind of honest, emotionally attuned reflection strengthens trust on both sides. When reflection replaces lecture, connection deepens. Your role shifts from enforcer to guide, from fixer to mentor. You're no longer the one handing down lessons; you're the one helping your loved one discover their own. This subtle shift communicates faith — faith in their ability to grow and in your ability to withstand the discomfort that comes with it.

Together, these steps — anticipating, communicating, holding steady, and reflecting — create a container strong enough to hold the weight of real learning. Within this structure, mistakes lose their sting. They become part of a predictable rhythm: choices, consequences, reflection, growth. The process itself becomes a teacher.

When done consistently, this approach changes the emotional climate of a family. Power struggles decrease, trust increases, and everyone begins to relax into their roles. The young person learns that their actions matter — that life responds not with punishment, but with feedback. The parent learns that love can hold boundaries without collapsing under guilt or fear.

In the end, creating safe containers for consequences is about more than managing behavior. it is about cultivating resilience — the ability to experience challenges without falling apart, to feel discomfort without losing connection. It is about teaching, through presence and consistency, that growth is not a solitary act but a shared journey — one held in the safety of a relationship.

When you can offer that kind of containment — steady, predictable, and compassionate — you become the emotional scaffolding that allows your loved one to build their own strength. And that, more than any punishment or rescue, is what leads to lasting change.

The Role of Emotional Safety

Natural consequences only lead to growth when they are experienced within the context of emotional safety. A young person cannot meaningfully reflect on their choices if they feel attacked, humiliated, or abandoned. When the body perceives threat — whether through raised voices, sarcasm, or cold withdrawal — the brain shifts from reflection to defense. The message received is not *"I'm learning something important,"* but *"I'm not safe."* Emotional safety is the invisible foundation on which all real learning rests. It is what allows discomfort to become tolerable and feedback to become useful. When a young person feels secure in the relationship — when they trust that love remains intact even when boundaries are enforced — their brain stays open and receptive. The prefrontal cortex, responsible for reasoning and insight, can stay online. They can think, feel, and process at the same time. Without that safety, consequences land as rejection rather than guidance, shame rather than structure.

For parents, this often requires unlearning old scripts about discipline. Many were raised to believe that consequences must be stern to be effective — that authority requires a certain edge, that "learning your lesson" should hurt a little. But modern neuroscience tells a different story. The brain learns best not in states of fear, but in states of safety. When the nervous system senses threat, the amygdala — the brain's alarm center — takes over, flooding the body with stress hormones. Reflection becomes impossible. Safety, not severity, is what makes lessons stick.

Tone and timing are the most powerful tools a parent has in creating emotional safety. The same words can teach or wound depending on how and when they are delivered. A calm, steady voice communicates respect and stability. A sarcastic or frustrated tone — even if the words are reasonable — communicates shame. Timing matters too. Consequences delivered in the heat of conflict are rarely absorbed. When emotions are high, both parent and loved one are operating from their limbic system — reactive, defensive, impulsive. Nothing constructive happens there.

A simple phrase can change the entire dynamic: *"Let's talk when we have both had a chance to breathe."* This line does more than delay an argument; it models self-regulation. It tells your loved one, *"I respect you enough to wait until we can both listen."* That small act of restraint conveys trust — not only in your loved one's ability to calm down, but in your own. It transforms a potential power struggle into a moment of modeling emotional maturity. When you return to the conversation after calm has been restored, the tone of the exchange changes entirely. Instead of tension, there is space. Instead of defensiveness, there is curiosity. The teenager or young adult may still resist, minimize, or deflect, but beneath that surface, they will experience something powerful: safety. They know that your love isn't contingent on perfection, and that their mistakes don't erase their belonging. This emotional security becomes the soil where responsibility can grow.

In families navigating substance use or mental-health challenges, emotional safety is often the first casualty and the most important repair. Crises can make communication reactive; fear and frustration can turn even gentle parents into investigators or enforcers. Restoring safety means slowing down enough to rebuild trust. It means shifting from interrogation to invitation — from *"Why would you do that?"* to *"Help me understand what was happening for you."* This kind of language tells your loved one that they are seen, not judged.

Emotional safety does not mean avoiding hard truths or minimizing impact. It means delivering truth with steadiness and empathy. You can say, *"This behavior can't continue,"* without raising your voice. You can hold boundaries and love at the same time. The power of that combination is transformative — firm enough to provide containment, gentle enough to preserve connection. When safety is present, even painful consequences can become opportunities for insight. A young person who feels secure in the relationship can tolerate discomfort long enough to ask themselves, *"What did I learn from this?"* That moment of internal reflection is what builds self-awareness and accountability. Without safety, those same experiences harden into shame or defiance.

Parents often underestimate how much their emotional tone shapes the learning environment. Your calm body, steady voice, and willingness to pause are not small things — they are regulatory signals to your loved one's nervous system. You are communicating, *"We can handle this together."* Over time, this becomes an internalized voice for your loved one: the calm center they will one day call upon in moments of distress.

In this way, emotional safety is not only a tool for parenting — it is a legacy. It teaches loved one that love does not vanish when mistakes occur, that accountability does not require humiliation, and that repair is always possible. It models the kind of relationships they will someday create with others: those grounded in mutual respect, compassion, and emotional honesty. When parents lead with emotional safety, consequences become less about control and more about collaboration. The conversation shifts from punishment to partnership, from *"You need to learn your lesson"* to *"We're figuring this out together."* In that shared space — where calm meets compassion — accountability stops feeling like rejection and starts feeling like belonging.

That's where growth happens. That's where resilience begins. And that's where the heart of healing — for both parent and loved one — truly takes root.

Reflection & Practice

1. Identify one situation this week where your instinct is to rescue. Ask yourself: what might happen if I allow the natural consequence instead?

2. Practice saying: *"I'm here, and I trust you to figure this out."* Notice how it feels in your body — nervous, relieved, conflicted.

3. Reflect afterward: Did your loved one learn something meaningful? Did your anxiety decrease over time?

4. Journal about what this approach reveals — not just about your loved one's growth, but your own.

Chapter 6

Parenting Through Crisis

Crisis has a sound. It is the tremor in a parent's voice when the phone rings at midnight, the gasp when they find the text message, the pill bottle, or the note. The world narrows to one thought: *Please let them be okay.*

Every family walking the path of recovery or mental health challenges eventually faces moments like these. They arrive without warning, demanding instant action while your body floods with fear. You can't prevent every crisis — but you can learn how to move through it with steadiness and compassion.

Understanding Crisis

A crisis is not only an event — it is a *state of the nervous system*. It's what happens when emotional, physical, or psychological stress overwhelms a person's ability to cope. In those moments, everyone involved — parent, adolescent, young adult — becomes flooded with stress hormones like adrenaline and cortisol. The heart races, breathing quickens, muscles tighten. The body's entire system shifts from reflection to protection. The thinking brain — the prefrontal cortex — goes offline, and the survival brain takes over. Logic disappears; instinct takes the wheel.

For parents, this shift can be confusing and frightening. You may find yourself trying to reason, problem-solve, or lecture in the middle of chaos, wondering why nothing you say seems to land. But during a crisis, the part of the brain capable of processing language and perspective is largely inaccessible. Your loved one isn't ignoring you — they can't process new information. Their nervous system has been triggered into a defensive response. And often, without realizing it, so is yours.

When your loved one slams a door, screams, runs, or shuts down, they're communicating the only way their dysregulated nervous system knows how: *I'm overwhelmed; I don't feel safe.* Parents may mirror that energy — raising their voice, demanding explanations, pleading for calm. But what's really happening is two alarm systems reacting to each other. The result is escalation, not resolution. Communication collapses because everyone's physiology is on high alert.

Understanding this isn't about excusing behavior — it is about recognizing biology. In a crisis, no one is operating at full capacity. The goal isn't to make sense of what's happening or to fix it immediately; the goal is to stabilize the nervous system. When we understand that crisis is physiological, not moral, we stop taking reactions personally and start approaching them strategically.

In the heat of the moment, safety always comes before understanding. Trying to reason with someone in nervous system activation is like trying to have a conversation with a fire alarm — it is not built for dialogue; it is built for warning. The priority needs to become reducing intensity. Lowering your voice. Slowing your breathing. Using as few words as possible. Your calm presence becomes the anchor in the storm. When you regulate yourself, your nervous system sends a subtle but powerful message to theirs: *it is safe enough to come down.*

Sometimes, safety means physical containment — removing substances, separating people, calling for help, or stepping out of the room to prevent escalation. Other times, it means emotional containment — saying softly, *"I can see this is too much right now. Let's take a break and come back when we're calmer."* This simple act can prevent a full spiral by acknowledging the reality of the moment: no one can think clearly when their body believes it is under threat. Once the immediate intensity passes, the body begins to recover. Breathing slows, adrenaline fades, and the thinking brain starts to come back online. Only then can reflection or conversation begin. Parents often rush this stage — eager to process, explain, or extract a promise that "it won't happen again." But the brain needs time to reset before it can engage meaningfully. The period immediately after a crisis is not for analysis; it is for grounding, rest, and reconnection.

When calm returns, understanding can follow. This is the moment for gentle curiosity — not *"Why did you do that?"* but *"What was happening for you when things got so intense?"* That shift in language signals safety and respect. It acknowledges that behavior is often communication — a signal of distress rather than defiance.

For families navigating substance use or co-occurring mental health challenges, crises may occur often — arguments over curfews, relapses, self-harm scares, or emotional shutdowns. Each one can feel like a personal failure or a sign of danger. But remembering that crisis is a nervous-system event, not a moral one, changes everything. It allows you to move from panic to purpose — from trying to control the storm to learning how to steady yourself within it. Approaching a crisis this way does not make it less painful, but it does make it less chaotic. It turns the focus from blame to regulation, from reaction to response. When parents can meet crises with composure — or at least awareness — they model what emotional stability looks like under stress. Over time, that modeling helps their loved one learn to do the same.

In the end, understanding the crisis is about humility. It is about recognizing that even in our most urgent moments, growth does not come from control but from containment. Safety comes first; meaning comes later. When you stop trying to solve a storm and start learning how to stand steady within it, you transform not just the crisis — but the family system itself.

The Crisis Compass: A Four-Step Framework

In the midst of a crisis, clarity evaporates. The human brain, flooded with fear and adrenaline, defaults to instinct. Parents often describe these moments as out-of-body experiences — everything happens fast, voices rise, hearts race, and reason disappears. Later, they replay every word, wondering if they could have done something differently. The truth is, in a crisis, *no one* communicates at their best. The key is not to eliminate panic, but to have a simple map — a framework that helps you stay oriented when the storm hits.

Think of this as your Crisis Compass — a four-step guide to help you ground, assess, contain, and reflect. It is not a script, but a way of thinking that turns chaos into structure. It acknowledges that a crisis is not only an event but a nervous-system storm — one that floods both parents and loved ones. These steps help you move from reactivity to regulation, from confusion to containment.

Step 1: Pause to Ground

Before speaking or moving, pause. One breath — that's all it takes to start shifting from instinct to awareness. In a crisis, your body wants to act immediately. You might feel the urge to shout, to run, to fix, to control. But if you respond before grounding, you will escalate rather than lower the emotional temperature.

Start with yourself: plant your feet firmly on the ground, unclench your hands, and take a slow, deep breath. Notice your heart rate. Feel the air entering and leaving your body. This is not a mindfulness exercise for its own sake — it is biology. When you slow your breathing, you send a direct signal to your nervous system that you are not in immediate danger. Your parasympathetic system — the body's "rest and restore" response — begins to activate.

Your calm physiology becomes contagious. The human nervous system is wired for co-regulation, meaning one person's calm can stabilize another's chaos. In those few seconds of stillness, you're not only grounding yourself — you're anchoring the entire moment. Before you say anything, ask yourself: *Am I responding to the crisis, or to my fear of it?*

Step 2: Assess Safety

Once you've grounded, shift your attention to immediate safety. This is where clarity matters most. Ask yourself three simple but crucial questions:

Is anyone in immediate danger?

Is there a medical risk — substance ingestion, self-harm, overdose, or violence?

Are emergency services needed?

If the answer to any of these questions is "yes," act without hesitation. Call 911, seek medical help, or involve professionals. In a true emergency, protection always comes before privacy or pride. Parents often fear that involving outside help will destroy trust — and in the short term, it might strain the relationship. But trust can be rebuilt; life cannot.

Err on the side of safety. It is better to over-respond once than to under-respond when it matters most. Afterward, when calm returns, you can explain your reasoning: *"I made the call because I love you and was scared for your safety. I know it might have felt invasive, but I couldn't take the risk of losing you."* Framed with honesty and compassion, even difficult interventions can become moments of truth, not betrayal.

Step 3: Contain the Situation

When the immediate danger has passed, the next goal is containment — not control, not correction. Containment is about reducing stimulation so that everyone's nervous system has a chance to settle. Think of it as turning down the volume on the environment and the emotions.

Start by softening the physical space. Lower your voice. Dim the lights. Reduce the number of people in the room. If multiple family members are shouting or panicking, calmly ask others to step out. Avoid interrogation — your loved one's brain is still in a defensive state, unable to process logic or absorb questions.

Simple, grounding statements work best. Say things like:

"You're safe."

"I'm here."

"We'll figure this out together."

These phrases bypass the rational mind and speak directly to the body. They tell your loved one that the threat has passed and that they are not alone. Even if they don't respond or appear dismissive, your calm words and tone are doing invisible work — signaling safety, modeling regulation, and creating space for de-escalation.

Containment also means containing *your own impulses*. Parents often want answers right away: *"What happened? Why did you do this?"* But in the heat of crisis, explanations are useless. The goal is to lower emotional intensity, not to resolve the issue. There will be time for understanding later — once everyone's nervous system has come back online.

Step 4: Reflect and Repair Later

After every storm comes a crash. Once the adrenaline fades, exhaustion sets in — for both parents and loved ones. This is the moment for reflection, not punishment. The crisis itself is over, but its meaning is still forming. What you say and do now shapes how your loved one will remember the event — as another episode of chaos or as the beginning of repair.

When calm returns, invite gentle reflection:
"What happened tonight?"
"What do you need to feel safe right now?"
"How can we plan to prevent this next time?"

These questions are not interrogations; they are invitations. They help your loved one shift from shame to insight. The goal isn't to assign blame but to build understanding. You might also share your own reflections: *"I was scared tonight. I wish I'd stayed calmer. Next time, I want us both to feel safer."* Modeling accountability — even in small ways — teaches far more than lectures ever could.

In this reflective stage, resist the temptation to rehash every detail or demand apologies. The nervous system learns best through compassion and repetition, not criticism. Reflection works when it is brief, calm, and consistent. Over time, these moments teach your loved one — and your family — that even crises can end with connection rather than disconnection.

Turning Crisis into Opportunity

When you move through these four steps — grounding, assessing, containing, and reflecting — crisis begins to transform. It becomes less of an unpredictable eruption and more of a process you can navigate. Each cycle teaches the nervous system resilience: *We can survive intensity without destruction. We can recover.*

Parents who practice this framework often notice subtle but powerful shifts. Arguments that once lasted hours de-escalate more quickly. Fear gives way to steadiness. Communication, once shattered by panic, becomes possible again. Over time, this consistency rewires the family system itself. The loved one's brain learns that emotion, even intense emotion, is not fatal — and the parent's brain learns that control is not the same as safety. The goal isn't to prevent every storm but to learn how to stand through it. When a crisis arises, you will have a compass. And with each use, you'll find that your family's collective nervous system becomes a little stronger, a little wiser, and a little more capable of finding its way back to calm.

Why Calm Is Contagious

In the midst of crisis or conflict, calm may feel like the least natural response — yet it is the most powerful one. Neuroscience tells us that emotional regulation isn't just personal; it is relational. Our nervous systems are designed to synchronize with those around us, especially in moments of threat or distress. This process, known as co-regulation, means that your calm — or your chaos — becomes your loved one's emotional weather.

When a parent enters a room with steady breath, grounded posture, and a gentle tone, something remarkable happens. The young person's body, even if flooded with stress hormones, begins to recalibrate. The heartbeat slows slightly. The muscles loosen. The breathing evens out. The message received isn't in words but in physiology: *You're safe enough to come down.* This is not a poetic metaphor — it is biology. The vagus nerve, which connects the brain to the body, plays a central role in regulating emotional states. When a parent's nervous system is calm, their facial expressions, voice tone, and breathing rhythm activate cues of safety in their loved one's nervous system. This response, sometimes called neuroception, happens below consciousness. The body recognizes safety before the mind does.

That's why, in moments of panic, *words matter less than energy.* A calm voice carries far more impact than a thousand urgent sentences. If your tone is steady, your loved one's brain begins to mirror that steadiness. If your tone is frantic, their alarm system stays online. In essence, your nervous system becomes the tuning fork that sets the frequency for the room.

Parents often underestimate their influence in a crisis. They assume that if they're not saying the perfect thing, they're failing. But what matters most is not the precision of your language — it is the regulation of your presence. Your calm breathing, your lowered shoulders, your softened eyes communicate something words can't: *We will survive this together.* Many parents mistake calm for indifference. They fear that if they don't show urgency, they'll appear not to care. But calm is not apathy — it is containment. It is the steady hand that holds the system together when everything else feels unstable. In families facing substance use or mental health challenges, this distinction is vital. When emotions run high, what the system needs most is an anchor — someone whose steadiness communicates, *We are not beyond repair.*

Think of calm as the emotional equivalent of oxygen. It does not remove the danger, but it makes it possible to breathe through it. A parent's regulated presence helps their loved one find footing in chaos. The young person may not respond right away — they may still yell, cry, or retreat — but their nervous system is registering your signal nonetheless. It is the light in the tunnel that says, *Follow me out.* The challenge, of course, is maintaining that calm when your own fear is spiking. Parents watching their loved one spiral into danger — intoxicated, withdrawn, or self-destructive — experience their own nervous-system storm. Their pulse races, their chest tightens, their brain floods with what-ifs. In those moments, calm is not instinctive; it is an act of discipline and love. It is saying to yourself, *My fear is real, but it does not get to drive.*

You don't need to feel calm to *be* calm. Regulation begins with awareness, not perfection. Taking one slow breath, loosening your jaw, or lowering your voice by one octave are all physiological cues that start to shift your body toward equilibrium. Each small act of regulation is a message to your loved one's nervous system: *We are safe enough to slow down.* Over time, this becomes a learned rhythm. The more consistently you bring calm into moments of intensity, the more your loved one's brain learns to borrow that steadiness. Eventually, they begin to internalize it — your calm becomes their calm. That's how co-regulation turns into self-regulation.

This is one of the quiet miracles of parenting through crisis. Even when you feel powerless to change your loved one's behavior, you hold immense influence over the emotional climate. You can't always stop the storm, but you can control the wind in your own sails. And that steady presence — grounded, compassionate, unshaken — becomes a lighthouse for your loved one, guiding them toward safety when they can't yet see it themselves.

Calm does not erase chaos, but it creates the space in which healing can begin. it is not the absence of fear — it is the decision to stay centered in the presence of it. In the language of the nervous system, calm says: *We're still connected. We're still here. And we will find our way through this together.*

After the Immediate Crisis

When the dust finally settles after a crisis, the silence that follows can feel almost as overwhelming as the chaos that came before it. The adrenaline that fueled survival begins to drain away, leaving behind exhaustion, confusion, and emotional whiplash. Parents often describe this period as standing in the wreckage — relieved that everyone is safe, but shaken by how quickly things spiraled. It is common to swing between relief and anger: *Thank God it is over* collides with *How did this happen again?* Both emotions are normal. Both are signs that your nervous system is coming down from high alert.

The body, much like the mind, needs time to reset. After a crisis, your system is still flooded with stress hormones. Sleep might feel impossible, your appetite may vanish, and your thoughts may race in loops of replay and regret. This is the aftershock period — the emotional echo of crisis. it is during this time that many parents rush to process what happened, to demand explanations or promises, or to put new rules in place. But what the nervous system truly needs first is rest. Before reflection comes regulation.

Take care of yourself first. This isn't indulgence; it is triage. Eat something nourishing, drink water, rest your body. Call your support network — a trusted friend, a therapist, a partner, or another parent who understands. Talk, cry, exhale. Do whatever helps you return to your baseline. You cannot guide recovery from depletion. A dysregulated parent cannot regulate a loved one. Your steadiness will be needed soon, but right now, it is okay to step away and breathe.

Once calm returns — for both you and your loved one — it is time for what clinicians call the debrief conversation. This conversation transforms crisis into understanding, but only when it happens from a place of regulation, not reactivity. The purpose is not to assign blame or deliver lectures, but to make meaning of what happened and plan for safety moving forward.

Start by revisiting the facts — briefly and without judgment. Stick to observable events, not emotional interpretations. For example: *"You drank, passed out, and we went to the hospital."* Simple, factual language reduces defensiveness and keeps the focus on reality rather than accusation. It reminds everyone that this is not a debate— it is a shared effort to understand what occurred.

Next, share your feelings using "I" statements. This models vulnerability without blame and helps your loved one see the emotional impact of their choices. *"I was terrified when I got that call."* Statements like this connect rather than divide. They shift the dynamic from *you versus me* to *us together in this experience.* Parents often fear that revealing emotion will make them seem weak or easily manipulated, but in truth, honesty builds empathy. It shows that boundaries and love can coexist.

Then, explore causes — gently, with curiosity rather than interrogation. Ask questions that invite reflection:

"What was happening before you decided to drink?"

"Were you feeling pressure, sadness, or something else?"

The goal here is to understand context, not to extract confession. When young people feel heard rather than judged, they are far more likely to identify the emotions or triggers beneath their behavior. These insights often reveal the underlying pain — loneliness, anxiety, shame — that drives risky choices.

Finally, collaborate on next steps. Crisis becomes an opportunity for healing when parents and a loved one work together on solutions. Instead of dictating consequences or treatment plans in isolation, engage together in problem-solving:

"Let's decide together what kind of support feels right."

"Would you be open to talking with someone — maybe a counselor or therapist?"

Collaboration communicates respect and reinforces agency. It tells your loved one, *"You are not powerless in your recovery."* Even if they resist or minimize, the act of including them lays the groundwork for future cooperation.

The aftermath of a crisis is also a chance for repair. If you said or did things you regret in the heat of the moment, name them. Repair does not require elaborate apologies — just honesty and humility:

"I wish I had stayed calmer last night. I was scared and overreacted."

When parents model accountability, they teach it. Repairing your own mistakes shows your loved one that relationships can survive rupture — that love does not disappear when people struggle.

This period can also bring up deeper layers of grief. Many parents report feeling haunted by the gap between the loved one they imagined and the one standing before them. Allow yourself to mourn that quietly if you need to. Grief is part of healing. It softens the rigid edges of anger and makes space for compassion.

Remember, crisis recovery is not a single conversation — it is a process. Your loved one may not respond the way you hope. They may deny, deflect, or retreat. That's okay. The goal is not immediate insight; it is consistency. Keep showing up calmly, holding boundaries, and communicating care. Over time, the repetition of safe, honest conversations teaches more than any one talk ever could.

Above all, give yourself grace. Parenting through crisis is one of the most difficult emotional experiences imaginable. There are no perfect responses — only the ongoing practice of returning to steadiness, empathy, and hope. Each time you pause instead of panic, listen instead of lecture, reflect instead of react, you're impacting not only your family's dynamics but you are also rewiring your own nervous system toward resilience.

When the next crisis comes — and inevitably, another wave will — you'll find that your foundation is stronger. The body remembers safety. The heart remembers the connection. And each recovery makes the next one a little more possible.

When to Seek Professional Help

Every family reaches a point where love and patience, though essential, are not enough on their own. Crisis, especially when it repeats or escalates, is often a sign that more structure and professional support are needed. Yet for many parents, recognizing this can feel like crossing an critical threshold — one that carries guilt, fear, and sometimes shame. Seeking help may stir painful questions: *Did I fail? Should I have seen this coming? What will people think?*

It is important to remember that treatment is not a punishment; it is protection. It is a form of care that extends the circle of safety beyond the home. When a young person's emotional or behavioral struggles exceed what a family can manage alone, reaching out for help is not a sign of weakness — it is a profound act of strength. It means you're honoring the seriousness of what's happening and creating the conditions where healing can occur. Parents often hesitate to involve professionals because they worry about damaging trust. They fear that suggesting therapy, hospitalization, or a treatment program will make their loved one feel labeled or abandoned. But when presented calmly and compassionately, professional help communicates the opposite message: *You are not beyond help, and we are not beyond hope.* It says, *This is too big for us to carry alone, but we'll carry it together — with the right people beside us.*

There are several moments when professional involvement becomes not just helpful, but necessary.

1. Safety cannot be maintained at home.

If you find yourself constantly on alert — hiding medications, locking up alcohol, staying awake at night to monitor your loved one — the family system has moved into survival mode. This level of hypervigilance is unsustainable and unsafe for everyone involved. When you can no longer guarantee physical or emotional safety within the household, it is time to bring in outside support. A therapist, psychiatrist, or crisis service can assess risk and help determine whether a higher level of care (such as a partial hospitalization or residential program) is appropriate.

2. The same crisis repeats without progress.

Patterns tell a story. When similar incidents — intoxication, outbursts, self-harm threats, or disappearances — occur again and again despite conversation and boundary-setting, it suggests that the underlying issue hasn't been addressed. Repetition means the coping strategies available to your loved one (and to you) are no longer sufficient. Professional help brings fresh perspective and new tools. It helps break the cycle by identifying what's driving the behavior beneath the surface.

3. Substance use escalates beyond your ability to monitor.

It is one thing to suspect occasional experimentation; it is another to face clear signs of dependence — missing substances, withdrawal symptoms, lying, or increased isolation. Parents are not equipped to manage detoxification or medical risks at home. Substance use disorders change brain chemistry, impulse control, and emotional stability. In these cases, structured intervention isn't about discipline — it is about safety and stabilization. Clinical programs offer medical oversight, accountability, and therapeutic containment that families cannot replicate on their own.

4. Self-harm or suicidal thoughts are disclosed.

This is always a red flag that requires immediate professional assessment. Even if your loved one insists that they were "just joking" or "didn't mean it," these statements should never be ignored. Safety planning, evaluation by a mental health clinician, and sometimes hospitalization may be necessary to prevent tragedy. It is far better to over-respond than to risk under-responding when someone's life may be in danger. In these moments, calm firmness is crucial: *"I love you too much to ignore this. We need help right now."*

Professional help can take many forms, depending on the situation and severity. It may start with individual therapy, where your loved one works with a licensed clinician to explore emotions, behaviors, and triggers in a safe environment. Sometimes, family therapy or parent coaching is just as vital — giving parents tools to set boundaries, communicate effectively, and regulate their own nervous systems.

For some families, the next step might involve a psychiatric evaluation to assess whether medication could help stabilize mood, reduce anxiety, or manage underlying mental health conditions that may be fueling substance use. In more serious cases, intensive outpatient programs (IOPs), partial hospitalization programs (PHPs), or residential treatment centers may be recommended. These programs provide structured care — daily therapy, medical monitoring, and peer support — while helping young people practice new coping skills in real time.

Whatever the level of care, remember this: you are not sending your loved one *away* for treatment; you are sending them *toward* safety. Professional help does not replace parental love — it reinforces it. It provides what home cannot: neutral ground, trained eyes, and a system designed to contain what has become uncontainable within the family. You may also find that you, as a parent, need support during this transition. It is common to experience secondary trauma, anxiety, or burnout after months (or years) of crisis. Individual therapy, support groups, and family education programs can help you process your own emotions and strengthen your capacity to remain steady. Your wellbeing is not secondary — it is central to your loved one's recovery.

Seeking professional help is not the end of the road; it is the beginning of a different kind of journey — one where expertise, compassion, and structure converge to create a new possibility for healing. You are not alone in this process. Every day, families around the world make the same brave decision: to ask for help before it is too late.

Getting professional help does not mean you've failed. It means you've chosen to fight differently — with support, with boundaries, and with hope. And in the long run, that's the kind of strength that saves lives.

Avoiding Common Traps

In the emotional aftermath of a crisis, parents often find themselves reacting from instinct rather than intention. The fear of losing a loved one to substance use or mental illness is one of the deepest terrors a parent can experience, and fear has a way of distorting perception. It can make small issues feel catastrophic and serious ones feel impossible to face. In those moments, our nervous system reaches for control — through yelling, denial, or worst-case thinking. These reactions are deeply human, but they can also unintentionally make healing harder. Recognizing these patterns is not about blame; it is about reclaiming choice in moments that feel out of control.

There are three common traps families often fall into when trying to respond to a crisis: overreaction, underreaction, and catastrophizing. Each arises from love and fear intertwined — and each can be softened by awareness.

Overreaction: When Fear Becomes Fire

Overreaction is perhaps the most common response to a crisis. It can take the form of yelling, threatening, lecturing, or moralizing — often delivered in the language of desperation: *"What were you thinking?" "Do you want to destroy your life?" "If you ever do this again, you're out of this house!"* Underneath these words is not anger alone, but terror. The parent's body, flooded with adrenaline, is trying to regain control of what feels uncontrollable.

Yet when fear is expressed as fury, the message gets lost. What the young person hears is not *"I love you and I'm scared,"* but *"You are a disappointment and a danger."* Shame floods in, and shame rarely leads to change. Instead, it drives secrecy, denial, or defiance. Overreaction teaches the nervous system that connection is unsafe — that crisis equals rejection.

In moments of intensity, remember that calm does not mean condoning. You can express seriousness without aggression. Statements like, *"I can't let this continue be-*

cause I care about you too much to pretend it is okay," communicate boundaries and love simultaneously.

Underreaction: When Fear Disguises Itself as Calm

On the other end of the spectrum lies underreaction — minimizing, rationalizing, or pretending the situation isn't serious. Parents sometimes do this because they are overwhelmed, or because they hope denial will make the problem disappear. It can sound like, *"Everyone experiments,"* *"They just had a rough night,"* or *"I don't want to make things worse by overreacting."*

This form of protection often comes from exhaustion. After months or years of stress, the nervous system numbs itself as a form of survival. But underreaction sends a dangerous message: that risk is tolerable, or that the behavior isn't cause for alarm. Young people, especially those struggling with substance use or mental health issues, are highly attuned to what their parents do, not what they say. If parents avoid addressing the issue, it can reinforce denial — *"See, it is not that bad."*

Acknowledging seriousness does not have to mean panicking. It means stating the truth clearly and compassionately: *"What happened tonight was serious. We need to talk about how to make sure it does not happen again."* Calm acknowledgment is often more powerful than emotional intensity. It shows your loved one that you're capable of handling the situation without collapsing or attacking — and that's what makes safety and accountability possible.

Catastrophizing: When Fear Becomes the Future

Catastrophizing happens when a parent's imagination runs ahead of the facts. It sounds like, *"You're going to ruin your life," "You'll never recover from this,"* or *"If this keeps up, you'll end up dead."* These statements come from love twisted by fear — the desperate attempt to make a young person see the stakes. But instead of motivating change, catastrophizing often creates paralysis. When a young person feels their future is already doomed, hope collapses. The brain interprets catastrophic statements as proof that there's no way back — that the damage is permanent. And when hope disappears, so does the motivation to try.

The truth is that recovery rarely follows a straight line, and even serious mistakes do not define a life. Parents who can hold a vision of possibility — *"You can come back from this. I believe in your ability to change"* — become powerful anchors of hope. Calm, realistic optimism is not naïve; it is neurologically reparative. It helps rewire the young person's sense of agency, replacing helplessness with possibility.

The Middle Path: Compassionate Accountability

Between overreaction and underreaction lies a quiet, steady middle ground — what therapists sometimes call *compassionate accountability*. It is the stance that says: *"I love you, and I take this seriously."* It balances empathy with structure, emotion with reason. It acknowledges the gravity of the situation without collapsing into panic or denial.

Compassionate accountability looks like calm acknowledgment of what happened, followed by clear boundaries and next steps. It sounds like: *"I know you're struggling. What happened tonight was dangerous, and we need to take steps to keep you safe. I'm not here to punish you — I'm here to help us move forward."* This approach keeps the focus where it belongs: on healing, not punishment. It allows consequences to be delivered without shame, and discussions to happen without hostility. When parents walk this middle path, they model the very skill their loved one needs most — the ability to stay regulated in the face of distress.

Over time, this balanced response rewires the family dynamic. The young person learns that love does not disappear during conflict, and the parent learns that calm is not weakness but leadership. Together, they begin to create a new emotional language — one rooted not in fear, but in faith: the quiet confidence that healing remains possible, even after the hardest nights.

The Gift Hidden in Crisis

In the moment, a crisis feels like destruction — the shattering of everything familiar. The phone call from the hospital, the night spent searching for your loved one, the trembling confrontation in the kitchen — these moments rupture a family's sense of safety and order. It is natural to see a crisis as failure, as the moment when everything you feared finally came true. But with time, and support, many families come to understand that a crisis is not an ending — it is also a beginning. Beneath the chaos, crisis carries information. It exposes what needs care, what has been avoided, and what is ready to change.

Every crisis reveals something essential about the family system. It shines light on unspoken dynamics, unacknowledged pain, or patterns that no longer serve anyone. Sometimes it reveals a gap in communication — how family members talk *around* the real issue instead of through it. Sometimes it exposes an emotional wound — a fear of abandonment, a history of trauma, or an inability to tolerate vulnerability. And sometimes it uncovers a truth that has been too painful to name: that love alone cannot heal what has not been addressed. When seen through this lens, crisis becomes feedback — an alarm, not a verdict. It does not announce that the family is broken beyond repair; it signals that something in the system needs attention. A crisis might be the moment when a young person's coping mechanisms finally collapse under pressure. Or it might be when a parent's capacity reaches its limit, forcing everyone to acknowledge that the current way of functioning isn't sustainable. In that sense, crisis is both devastating and clarifying. It demands that everyone stop pretending things are fine and begin the work of honest healing.

Parents who have weathered these storms often describe an unexpected shift once the initial shock passes. The masks fall away. Conversations that were once impossible become necessary. The language of survival gives way to the language of truth. One parent, reflecting after her daughter's overdose, said quietly, *"It broke us open. But it also made us real."* That sentence captures the paradox of crisis: it tears down the illusion of control, but in doing so, it creates the possibility of authenticity.

For many families, the greatest transformation comes not from the crisis itself, but from what follows — the willingness to tell the truth. Crisis strips away pretense. It asks, *What's really happening here? What are we avoiding? What needs to change, not just in my loved one, but in me?* These questions are painful, but they are also the doorway to growth. When a family can face them together, they often emerge more connected, more humble, and more attuned to one another's humanity.

In therapy, clinicians often talk about rupture and repair — the idea that healing does not come from avoiding breakdowns but from working through them with honesty and compassion. The same is true in families. A rupture — a crisis — does not destroy connection if it is followed by genuine repair. It can actually deepen trust.

Surviving a crisis with openness teaches everyone involved that love can stretch — that relationships can withstand truth, conflict, and even pain.

Seeing a crisis as feedback rather than failure also helps shift the emotional climate. Instead of blaming or collapsing into shame, families can approach crises with curiosity: *What is this moment trying to show us? What is being asked of us now?* This reframing does not erase the suffering, but it gives it purpose. It turns pain into data — information that can guide healing. Sometimes, the feedback is about communication: maybe conversations have been too reactive or too avoidant. Sometimes it is about boundaries: perhaps the family has confused love with rescue, or protection with control. And sometimes it is about emotional resilience — learning how to sit in discomfort without shutting down. Whatever the lesson, crisis invites growth by making what's hidden impossible to ignore.

The gift inside the crisis often emerges slowly, through reflection and distance. Months later, parents may look back and realize that the event that once terrified them also began to transform them. They might say, *"That was the moment we stopped hiding,"* or *"That was the night I realized I couldn't fix her, but I could still love her."* These realizations mark the turning points in family healing — the moments when control gives way to compassion, and fear begins to soften into acceptance.

It helps to remember that the word *crisis* comes from the Greek *krisis*, meaning "turning point" or "decision." It implies a crossroads — a moment when the old way must give way to something new. In this sense, crisis is not an interruption to the healing process; it *is* the process. It is the body, the family, and sometimes the universe saying, *you can't keep going like this.* it is the moment the system calls itself back into balance.

Families who choose to see crises this way discover resilience they didn't know they had. They learn that love does not mean preventing every breakdown, but staying present through them. They learn that strength does not come from control, but from connection. And they learn that the deepest repair often begins in the places where everything once seemed lost. When you can look at a crisis not as catastrophe, but as communication — not as a collapse, but as a call — it becomes a teacher. Painful, yes. Unwelcome, always. But also, profoundly instructive. It forces honesty, humility, and openness — the very ingredients that real recovery requires.

In time, what once felt like the end of the story can become the beginning of a truer one — the moment the family stopped performative survival and started living in truth. Crisis may break you open, but sometimes being broken open is the only way the light can get in.

Reflection & Practice

1. **Create your Crisis Compass.** Write down three steps you'll take the next time panic

strikes: who to call, what to say, how to ground yourself.

2. **Identify your personal anchors.** A phrase, object, or breathing pattern that calms you instantly — keep it accessible.

3. **Rehearse calm language.** Practice saying, "You're safe," or "I'm here," out loud until it feels natural.

4. **Plan for recovery after the crisis.** Who will you lean on? What support do *you* need? Parents heal too.

Chapter 7

Understanding Levels of Care

For many parents, the first signs of distress look deceptively manageable — a drop in grades, irritability, or a few missed curfews. You may think, *we'll talk about it this weekend,* or *once finals are over, things will calm down.* Then, slowly, the problem outgrows your comfort zone. A therapist recommends more support. Someone mentions "IOP" or "residential," and suddenly you're in a world that feels foreign and frightening.

Most parents have no roadmap for what comes next. Treatment language can sound like a foreign dialect — PHP, IOP, RTC, DBT, ASAM, dual-diagnosis, aftercare — all while you're still trying to process your loved one's pain.

This chapter is meant to translate that language, so that knowledge can become your anchor.

The truth is that recovery isn't one-size-fits-all. There is no single "right" program or perfect level of care — only the level that best matches your teen or young adult's current needs. Understanding the continuum of care will help you make decisions based not on fear or pressure, but on fit, safety, and timing.

Why Levels of Care Exist

Behavioral health treatment is organized into a *continuum* because people need different degrees of structure and support at different moments. The goal is not to escalate forever, but to find the least restrictive environment that still provides safety and meaningful progress.

Think of it like a series of steppingstones across a river. Each stone represents a level of care. The clinician's job is to determine which stone is sturdy enough to stand on right now — not the farthest one, and not the smallest one, but the next right one.

The Continuum of Care Explained

1. Outpatient Therapy (OP)

Structure: 1 or more individual sessions per week, sometimes concurrent with family therapy or parent coaching.

Best for: Early-stage experimentation with substances, emerging anxiety or depression, or as a maintenance phase after higher care.

Core Focus: Insight, coping skills, and communication.

Outpatient therapy is often the entry point — and for many teens and young adults, it works well. They keep living at home and attending school or work while receiving clinical support. The therapist functions like a compass, helping both adolescent and parent learn healthier emotional navigation.

But outpatient therapy can also plateau. If sessions start revolving around crisis control ("He was high again last weekend") rather than growth, that's a sign that structure needs to increase.

Parent reflection: Ask yourself, *Are we using therapy as an appropriate touch point, or as a life raft?* If it is the latter, you may be outgrowing the level.

2. Intensive Outpatient Program (IOP)

Structure: 3–5 days per week, 3 hours each day, combining group, individual, and family therapy.

Best for: Moderate substance use, co-occurring mental health challenges or mood instability, or a need for daily structure while remaining at home.

Core Focus: Accountability, relapse prevention, emotional regulation, and social learning.

An IOP is often the "sweet spot" between outpatient and full-time care. It allows your teen or young adult to stay integrated in school or work, while adding a therapeutic community and consistent oversight. The group element provides perspective and community — peers who "get it" can often reach your teen or young adult in ways parents cannot.

Parent role: Attend weekly family sessions. Reinforce at home what's being practiced in the program: open communication, boundaries, and consistent follow-through.

When done well, IOPs give adolescents and young adults a bridge — not a punishment — between outside challenges and sustainable change.

3. Partial Hospitalization Program (PHP)

Structure: 5 days per week, 5–6 hours daily, with psychiatric and medical oversight.
Best for: Escalating safety concerns, self-harm risk, severe mood symptoms, or repeated relapse after lower levels of care.
Core Focus: Stabilization — emotionally, behaviorally, and medically.

PHP is often described as a "day hospital." Clients return home in the evening but spend most of the day in a structured, therapeutic environment. This model works well when your loved one needs intensity but not 24-hour supervision.

4. Residential Treatment Center (RTC)

Structure: 24-hour supervised environment, typically 30–90 days (sometimes longer).
Best for: Chronic relapse, unsafe home dynamics, or co-occurring trauma and substance use requiring immersive support.
Core Focus: Safety, therapeutic immersion, and skill acquisition.

Residential programs vary widely — from hospital campuses to home-like environments — but all share one goal: stabilization through containment and healthy community. Clients step away from the triggers and routines that sustain maladaptive patterns.

Parents often fear this step most. It can feel like surrendering your role or "sending your loved one away." In reality, it is an expansion of your parenting — acknowledging that safety now requires a team.

Parent participation is critical: family therapy, weekly calls, and on-site workshops help maintain connection. Programs that include parent coaching during and after residential care tend to yield stronger reunification outcomes.

5. Wilderness and Experiential Programs

Structure: Outdoor or adventure-based therapeutic experiences, 6–12 weeks, combining nature immersion, group living, and therapy.
Best for: Resistance to traditional therapy, emotional dysregulation, or identity challenges.
Core Focus: Resilience, accountability, self-efficacy, and natural consequences.

The wilderness model leverages nature as both mirror and teacher. Adolescents or young adults who dismiss therapy in an office often connect differently when faced with real-world problem solving and physical challenges. Cooking over a fire, hiking through weather, and working with a team demand authenticity.

Critics sometimes question the intensity or cost, but research increasingly supports experiential approaches for certain populations — particularly those struggling with motivation, self-esteem, or trust in adults.

Parent involvement: letter-writing, coaching calls, and detailed family reunification planning. The transition home is as important as the experience itself.

6. Transitional and Sober Living

Structure: Semi-independent housing with staff supervision and therapeutic accountability.

Best for: Post-residential or young adult and older clients building life skills and relapse prevention.

Core Focus: Reintegration — balancing independence with community and structure.

Transitional living often bridges the gap between treatment and full independence. Young adults practice managing time, employment, and peer relationships while staying connected to therapeutic oversight. Think of it as "training wheels" for adulthood — not institutional, but intentional.

Choosing the Right Fit

Choosing the right level of care for your teen or young adult is one of the most difficult decisions a parent can make. It is not only a clinical judgment — it is an emotional leap. In many ways, it asks you to surrender the illusion of control and to trust a process that feels uncertain. Parents often describe this decision as a tug-of-war between fear and love: *Are we overreacting? Are we doing too much? What if they hate us for this?*

These are not trivial questions. They come from the ache of wanting to protect your loved one without losing their trust, of wanting to act without feeling like you've betrayed them. Every parent fears that taking the next step — whether it is suggesting therapy, arranging an evaluation, or enrolling in a treatment program — might push their loved one further away. But it is important to remember that intervention and love are not opposites. The most loving act, at times, is the one that sets a limit, introduces structure, and asks for help.

Clinically, the decision to increase the level of care should rest on three essential pillars: safety, functioning, and support. Together, they form a simple but powerful framework for determining when home-based management is no longer enough.

1. Safety: Is Your Teen or Young Adult Safe at Home Right Now?

This question comes first because it overrides all others. Safety means more than the absence of immediate danger — it includes emotional, physical, and environmental stability. Is your loved one safe with themselves and others? Are they using substances or behaviors in ways that pose risk for overdose or harm? Are they expressing suicidal thoughts, self-injurious behaviors, or aggression?

When safety cannot be guaranteed, the home environment — no matter how loving — becomes insufficient as the primary container. Parents often struggle here, torn between fear of institutionalization and the hope that things will stabilize on their own. But safety crises are not moral failures; they are medical emergencies. Just as you wouldn't hesitate to seek urgent care for a broken bone, you shouldn't hesitate to pursue professional stabilization for emotional or behavioral risk. Treatment in these moments isn't punishment — it is protection. It creates space for survival first, healing second.

2. Functioning: Can They Manage the Tasks of Daily Life?

The next indicator is functioning — how your teen or young adult is managing the ordinary demands of life. Can they attend school or work regularly? Are they completing tasks, maintaining friendships, and engaging in activities that once mattered to them?

When functioning breaks down — when sleep patterns invert, grades collapse, hygiene deteriorates, or isolation deepens — it signals that the internal distress has outpaced available coping skills. Functioning is like the canary in the coal mine; when it falters, it is a sign that deeper support is needed. Parents sometimes misread functional decline as laziness or defiance, but often it is neither. it is the body and mind saying, *I can't hold this anymore.*

If your loved one's functioning is significantly impaired despite ongoing support — if they can't meet basic expectations without constant crisis management — it is time to consider a more structured level of care. Programs like intensive outpatient (IOP) or partial hospitalization (PHP) are designed for this space: too complex for once-a-week therapy, but not requiring full residential treatment.

3. Support: Can You Provide the Containment They Need?

The final question is about you — your capacity, resources, and support system. Parents often underestimate how much this variable matters. Healing environments depend as much on the stability of the caregivers as on the condition of the loved one.

Ask yourself honestly: Do I have the bandwidth, emotional regulation, and resources to maintain consistency right now? Do I feel constantly on edge, walking on eggshells, or living in a state of crisis management? Are other family members, siblings, or partners being affected?

When the family system becomes stretched to the point of collapse, it is not sustainable for anyone. This does not mean you've failed — it means you've reached the natural limits of what love alone can hold. A higher level of care can provide the containment that the family no longer can, giving everyone space to reset.

When Two or More of These Areas Are Compromised

If two or more of these domains — safety, functioning, or support — are significantly impaired, it is time to step up care. This threshold isn't a judgment on your family; it is an act of protection. The goal is to match the *intensity* of care to the *intensity* of need. In the same way medical providers escalate treatment based on symptom severity, mental health professionals use structured criteria to guide these decisions.

Clinicians often reference the **ASAM Criteria** (American Society of Addiction Medicine), a framework used to evaluate risk and recommend appropriate levels of care. It looks across six dimensions:

Withdrawal potential – Are there medical risks related to substance use or discontinuation?

Biomedical conditions – Are there coexisting medical issues that complicate treatment?

Emotional, behavioral, or cognitive conditions – Are there mental health symptoms that interfere with functioning?

Readiness to change – How motivated is the person for recovery?

Relapse potential – How likely are they to return to use or harmful behaviors without containment?

Recovery environment – Is the home environment supportive or destabilizing?

Parents don't need to memorize or master this model. What matters is its spirit: match intensity to need, not to comfort. The goal isn't to choose the least disruptive option, but the most effective one. A decision rooted in fear of disruption — *"We don't want to scare them"* — can inadvertently delay safety and healing.

Balancing Emotion and Evidence

Every treatment decision sits at the intersection of emotion and evidence. Emotion says, *I'm scared.* Evidence says, *This situation meets the threshold for more care.* Neither voice should be ignored. The key is to let data guide the direction, and compassion shape the delivery. When you decide to pursue higher care, communicate openly and calmly with your loved one. Frame the choice as an act of care rather than control:

"We have tried what we can at home, and it is not working. You deserve more support than we can provide right now. This isn't a punishment — it is a step toward healing."

Even if they react with anger or disbelief, your consistency matters more than their immediate acceptance. Many young people resist at first — not because they don't need help, but because they fear judgment or loss of autonomy. In time, most recognize that structure was the very thing that made healing possible.

Finding the Right Balance

Choosing a level of care isn't a one-time decision — it is a process of calibration. The right fit might change as your loved one grows, stabilizes, or encounters new challenges. What begins as residential care may transition into out-patient therapy; what starts with crisis stabilization may evolve into long-term family work. The guiding principle is adaptability — responding to what's needed now, not what feels easiest or most familiar.

When parents can approach these decisions with both courage and compassion, something powerful happens. The loved one feels held — not in control of every out-come, but safely contained by a system that is steady, loving, and proactive. The parent feels grounded — not perfect or fearless, but confident that they are making choices aligned with safety and healing.

Choosing the right fit is not about doing it "right." It is about doing it *realistically and relationally.* It is the moment you move from crisis reaction to intentional care, from firefighting to fire prevention. And that shift — quiet, deliberate, courageous — is one of the most important steps on the family's path toward recovery.

Talking with Your Teen or Young Adult

Even when the clinical path forward is clear — when the signs of crisis, burnout, or substance use are unmis-takable — having the conversation about treatment is one of the hardest moments for any parent. You may know in your heart that more help is needed, but translating that conviction into words that your teen or young adult can hear without feeling blamed or betrayed takes care and intention.

The way you frame treatment matters as much as the decision itself. For your loved one, this conversation isn't just about logistics — it is about identity, autonomy, and trust. They may hear *"You need treatment"* as *"You've failed."* They may interpret your concern as control or rejection. That's why tone and pacing matter. You're not just conveying information; you're shaping the emotional climate that will determine how the next phase of healing begins.

Parents often come to this conversation exhausted — emotionally spent from sleepless nights, fear, and repeated attempts to hold things together. it is natural to feel urgent, to want to *make* your loved one understand the seriousness of the situation. But urgency and love can sound similar in tone and feel very different to a young person's nervous system. What you mean as care may land as criticism; what you intend as support may register as threat. The goal is to communicate seriousness without shame, structure without control. Begin with compassion and shared reality. A simple, grounding statement such as: *"We love you, and we can see how hard things have been. We think it is time to bring in more support — a team that can help you feel safe and get back to yourself."*

This approach does three things at once. It names love first, establishing emotional safety. It acknowledges struggle without judgment, validating your loved one's pain. And it frames treatment as collaboration, not coercion. The message is not *"You're broken and need fixing,"* but *"You're hurting, and you deserve more help than we can give."* That subtle shift changes everything.

Avoid framing treatment as an ultimatum or threat. Statements like, *"If you don't go, we're done helping,"* may come from desperation, but they communicate conditional love and heighten shame. For a teen or young adult already struggling with fear, guilt, or self-doubt, ultimatums can trigger resistance and rebellion. They also reinforce the idea that help equals control — that treatment is something being done *to* them, rather than *for* them.

Instead, emphasize partnership. Treatment works best when it is grounded in collaboration, not compliance. You can say,

"We want to find the right fit together — a place or a team that feels supportive and respectful. This is about helping you regain your footing, not taking away your freedom."

Even if your loved one disagrees or reacts angrily, stay anchored. Anger, denial, and deflection are often expressions of fear. They're signs of a nervous system trying to protect itself from shame or loss of control. When you remain calm, you communicate safety: *"We can handle this together, even when you're upset."*

This does not mean allowing disrespect or endless debate. It means staying regulated enough to hold both firmness and empathy at once. If the conversation escalates, it is okay to pause:

"I can see this feels overwhelming. Let's take a break and talk again later."

Pausing does not mean backing down; it means protecting the relationship from reactivity. It teaches your loved one that difficult conversations don't have to end in rupture — they can end in breathing space.

Remember that buy-in takes time. Many adolescents and young adults resist treatment at first, not because they don't need it, but because they fear what it represents: loss of independence, exposure of shame, or the stigma attached to needing help. Trust that these feelings will soften once safety and respect are established in the treatment environment. The job of the parent is not to convince, but to invite — not to force compliance, but to create conditions for willingness.

When emotions run high, focus less on persuasion and more on presence. You might not have all the right words, but your energy — calm, loving, grounded — speaks louder than any argument. The nervous system of a distressed young person looks for cues of safety in the parent's face, tone, and breathing. Your steadiness tells them: *"We're not in danger. We're in transition."* You can acknowledge their emotions without absorbing them. If they yell, *"You're ruining my life!"* you might respond, *"I hear how angry you are. I'd feel that way too if I thought someone was making decisions for me. But I want you to know this isn't about control — it is about care."* Naming the feeling without reacting to it helps defuse intensity. It shows that the relationship can hold big emotions without breaking.

Even in resistance, something powerful is happening: your loved one is witnessing your consistency. You are modeling what healthy regulation looks like under stress. Over time, that steadiness becomes internalized — your calm becomes their compass.

Talking about treatment is not a one-time conversation; it is an ongoing dialogue. You may need to revisit it several times, each time layering more understanding, more trust, and less fear. The goal isn't immediate agreement, but gradual acceptance. Each respectful conversation plants a seed that says, *"You're not alone in this."*

In families navigating substance use or mental health challenges, the path forward rarely looks smooth. But every step toward help — even the messy, tearful ones — is movement toward safety. When you approach this moment with clarity, compassion, and conviction, you offer your loved one something more powerful than persuasion: you offer them your calm belief that healing is possible.

Your words matter, yes. But your presence — steady, loving, and unshaken — is what opens the door.

Evaluating Programs

Finding the right program for your teen or young adult can feel like standing at the edge of a maze. There are countless options — residential treatment centers, therapeutic boarding schools, wilderness programs, partial hospitalization programs (PHPs), intensive outpatient programs (IOPs), and more. Each one claims expertise, compassion, and success. Their websites feature smiling faces, tranquil campuses, and words like *healing, hope,* and *transformation.* But behind the language and imagery, quality varies widely.

A glossy brochure or polished website does not guarantee excellence. The most effective programs are not always the most visually impressive — they are the ones that prioritize transparency, family inclusion, and individualized care. In truth, the best indicator of a strong program is not its marketing but its willingness to have honest, detailed conversations with you. When you ask questions, listen not just to *what* they say, but to *how* they respond. Do they sound patient or defensive? Do they welcome your curiosity or rush you toward a decision? Your intuition about tone and responsiveness is often as important as the information itself.

Choosing a program is both a clinical and relational decision. Clinically, you want to ensure the program has the right structure and resources to meet your loved one's needs. Relationally, you want to feel that the staff will treat your family with dignity and care. The following ten questions are designed to help you assess both.

1. How Are Family Sessions Structured?

Recovery does not happen in isolation. Effective programs recognize that healing within the family system is essential. Ask how often family therapy occurs, who facilitates it, and what topics are covered. Do they include siblings or extended family when appropriate? Is the approach focused on blame, or on communication and boundary repair?

Programs that treat parents as partners — rather than obstacles — foster long-term success. If family involvement feels tokenized or optional, that's a red flag.

2. How Do You Integrate Treatment for Co-Occurring Disorders?

Many young people struggling with substance use also experience anxiety, depression, trauma, ADHD, or other mental health conditions. The term *co-occurring disorders* refers to this overlap. Ask how the program addresses both issues simultaneously. Are there licensed clinicians trained in trauma-informed and evidence-based modalities such as DBT, CBT, or EMDR? How do they coordinate care between substance-use specialists and mental health professionals?

A program that siloes these issues — treating "addiction first, emotions later" — risks missing the root cause of the behavior. True recovery integrates both.

3. How Are Treatment Plans Individualized?

Each person's story is unique. A one-size-fits-all model rarely works, especially for adolescents and young adults. Ask how treatment plans are created and reviewed. What assessments do they use? How often is progress revisited? How does the team adapt when a client's needs shift?

Listen for words like *collaboration, customization,* and *flexibility.* A strong program views each client as an individual, not a diagnosis.

4. How Do You Handle Medication Management and Communication with Prescribers?

If your loved one is taking psychiatric medication — or may need to — clarity here is crucial. Who oversees medication management? Is there a psychiatrist or psychiatric nurse practitioner on staff? How often do they meet with clients? How are medication changes communicated with families and outpatient prescribers?

A reputable program will have clear, ethical guidelines around informed consent, safety monitoring, and communication. Vague or evasive answers can indicate disorganization or lack of clinical depth.

5. How Do You Define and Measure Progress?

"Progress" can mean many things — reduced substance use, improved mood regulation, better communication, restored trust. Ask the program to define how they measure change. What tools or indicators do they use? How do they distinguish between compliance (following rules) and internalization (genuine growth)?

A good program understands that healing is nonlinear. They'll talk about process, not perfection. If the emphasis feels overly behavioral or punitive — focused only on rules and consequences — the approach may lack psychological depth.

6. What Credentials Do Staff Hold, and What Is the Staff-to-Client Ratio?

Credentials matter. Ask who provides therapy — licensed clinicians (LCSWs, LPCs, LMFTs, LMHCs, PHDs, PsyDs) or paraprofessionals? What is the ratio of clinical staff to clients? How much time do clients actually spend with licensed providers each week? High-quality programs maintain reasonable ratios and invest in ongoing staff training and supervision.

7. How Do You Ensure Cultural Competence and Inclusivity?

Every family brings its own cultural, racial, gender, and spiritual context. Ask how the program ensures inclusivity in staff training, group facilitation, and treatment design. Do they have clinicians from diverse backgrounds? How do they address issues like identity, privilege, and bias within the therapeutic process?

Cultural humility is a marker of quality care. A program that welcomes this conversation — rather than skirting it — shows integrity and awareness.

8. What Aftercare or Alumni Support Do You Offer?

The end of treatment is not the end of recovery. Sustained change requires structure and community beyond discharge. Ask what transition planning looks like: Do they offer step-down programs, alumni groups, or family support after discharge? How do they help connect your loved one with outpatient providers?

A strong program will begin planning for aftercare early — sometimes from day one — recognizing that continuity of care prevents relapse and supports long-term growth.

9. How Often Will I Hear from My Teen or Young Adult's Therapist?

Regular communication between the treatment team and parents builds trust and alignment. Ask how often you'll receive updates and from whom. Will you have scheduled family calls or progress summaries? Are there boundaries around contact that support therapeutic goals while keeping you informed?

Transparency is key. You should never feel like you're in the dark. The best programs strike a balance between client privacy and family involvement.

10. How Do You Involve Parents in Transition Planning?

Transition is one of the most vulnerable stages in recovery. Relapse or regression often occur not during treatment, but after discharge — when structure fades and real-world stressors return. Ask how the program prepares both your loved one and your family for this phase. Do they facilitate family meetings, provide written plans, and identify local supports? Are you given guidance on how to set boundaries and expectations when your loved one returns home?

Programs that include parents in transition planning honor the truth that recovery is relational. They understand that family readiness is as important as client readiness.

Putting It All Together

A program that welcomes these questions — and answers them transparently — is a program that values partnership. Look for teams that invite dialogue, encourage second opinions, and provide references from alumni families. Trust professionals who communicate both confidence and humility — who can say, "Here's what we do well," and "Here's what might not fit for your loved one."

Above all, trust your intuition. If something feels off — rushed, defensive, or too good to be true — pause. The right program will never pressure you to decide out of fear. They will invite you to decide from informed hope.

Choosing care is an act of both discernment and faith. You are not just selecting a service — you're choosing an environment that will hold your loved one's most vulnerable self. When you approach this decision with clarity and curiosity, you send a quiet but powerful message: *Our family leads with love, and we are building a team that does the same.*

There are also professionals - educational consultations, family navigators, case managers, etc. - who can also help you navigate the landscape of treatment options to handpick ones that fit your loved one's needs and take the burden off of you to sift through the options.

Understanding Cost and Insurance

The financial side of treatment can feel overwhelming — and, for many families, it is one of the most stressful parts of the recovery journey. Just when emotions are already stretched thin, you're suddenly navigating a maze of deductibles, preauthorizations, and billing codes. It can feel like you've stepped into a foreign language at the exact moment you're least equipped to translate it. But while the system is complicated, there are ways to move through it strategically — and you don't have to do it alone.

Every program structures payment differently. Some accept in-network insurance, which typically means your plan has a direct agreement with the provider and a portion of costs are covered according to your policy. Others accept out-of-network benefits, where reimbursement occurs after you pay upfront and submit claims. Still others operate as private-pay programs, where fees are paid directly by families without insurance involvement.

It is easy to assume that one model automatically signals higher quality — that "private pay" must mean better care, or that "in-network" means limited support. The truth is more nuanced. There are excellent programs across all financial models. What matters most is fit, transparency, and integrity — not the billing category. A small, in-network community program can provide remarkable individualized care, just as a private-pay residential center can offer specialized expertise. Try not to let financial structure become a proxy for quality.

When the Jargon Hits

Unfortunately, the vocabulary of healthcare tends to appear at the worst possible moment — in crisis. Words like *deductible, utilization review, prior authorization,* and *single-case agreement* can sound intimidating, especially when you're also trying to secure help quickly. Understanding a few key concepts can make the process less overwhelming.

Deductible: The amount you must pay out of pocket before insurance begins covering services. Some plans have separate deductibles for in-network and out-of-network care.

Utilization Review: The process by which the insurance company reviews clinical documentation to determine whether a specific level of care (such as residential treatment or intensive outpatient) is justified.

Prior Authorization: A requirement that approval must be obtained *before* services begin. Without this, even medically necessary care may not be reimbursed.

Single-Case Agreement (SCA): A special contract between your insurance company and a program that's technically out of network. SCAs are sometimes approved when a particular type of care or specialization isn't available in-network.

These terms may feel like barriers, but they are simply part of the system's structure. Understanding them helps you advocate effectively — and advocacy is key.

Ask for a Case Manager

Most reputable programs have a dedicated insurance or admissions specialist who serves as a case manager. This person can help you navigate authorizations, communicate with the insurance company, and submit clinical documentation. Use them. They are your translator and advocate within the system.

Ask specifically:

"Who on your team handles insurance communication? How often will they update me? What documentation will you provide?"

A good program will have clear answers — and a clear process — for these questions.

Document Everything

Keep a record of every call, email, and clinical update. Documentation matters because insurance companies often require proof that a certain level of care is "medically necessary." Save discharge summaries, emergency room notes, and treatment reports from prior programs. These details provide evidence that higher levels of support are justified.

Consider creating a simple binder or digital folder with tabs for "Assessments," "Treatment Notes," and "Insurance Correspondence." Organized documentation not only strengthens your case but also reduces stress when you need to reference specific dates or outcomes.

Clarify "Medical Necessity"

Of all the terms in behavioral healthcare, this one carries the most weight. Coverage hinges on "medical necessity." It is the criterion insurers use to decide whether a given level of treatment — inpatient, residential, or outpatient — is justified.

Programs must demonstrate that the individual's symptoms, behaviors, or environment pose enough risk that lower levels of care would be ineffective or unsafe. For example, inability to maintain sobriety despite outpatient support, suicidal ideation, or medical complications from substance use all typically meet the threshold.

Ask the treatment program how they document and communicate medical necessity to insurers. The stronger and more consistent the clinical documentation, the more likely coverage will be approved or extended.

Seek Advocacy

You do not have to face insurance appeals or denials alone. National organizations such as the Partnership to End Addiction, NAMI (National Alliance on Mental Illness), and Mental Health America offer resources, hotlines, and template letters for appealing insurance denials.

Some families also work with independent patient advocates or behavioral health consultants who specialize in navigating coverage disputes. These professionals understand insurer language and can help draft appeals that speak directly to medical necessity.

If you encounter a denial, don't assume it is final. Denials are often overturned when additional clinical information is submitted. Persistence and clarity can make the difference between rejection and approval.

Don't Give Up After the First "No"

One of the most disheartening moments for parents is hearing, "Your plan won't cover that." But that response is rarely the end of the story. Many families eventually obtain coverage through appeals, peer-to-peer reviews, or single-case agreements. Insurance companies count on fatigue; persistence is your power.

Ask the program to help you request a peer-to-peer review, where your loved one's clinician speaks directly with the insurance company's medical reviewer to advocate for continued or higher care. These conversations often lead to reversals. Keep every denial letter and note the timelines for filing appeals — missing a deadline can forfeit your right to challenge the decision.

Exploring Financial Aid and Alternatives

If insurance coverage falls short, don't assume all options are out of reach. Many programs offer sliding scale fees, payment plans, or scholarship funds supported by private foundations. Some nonprofit treatment centers partner with local agencies or receive state funding to offset costs for qualifying families.

Ask directly:

"Do you have any financial aid programs or grants available? Are there foundations you partner with that support treatment access?"

You may be surprised by what's possible once you ask — and persist. In some cases, programs can help families secure state-sponsored funding or bridge grants designed specifically for adolescents and young adults in crisis.

Managing the Emotional Side of Finances

It is normal for financial stress to stir guilt, anger, or despair. Parents often say, *"We'd do anything for our loved one,"* and then feel crushed when resources are finite. Remember: financial limitations are not moral failures. They are realities of a complex system that even professionals find difficult to navigate. What matters most is your commitment to seeking help — not the price tag of the program you can afford.

Your advocacy itself is a form of care. By staying engaged, asking questions, and documenting your efforts, you are demonstrating to your loved one that recovery is worth fighting for — that their life is worth persistence.

The Parent's Inner Journey

Every logistical decision in the treatment process carries an invisible emotional weight. Behind every phone call, insurance form, and packing list lies a deeper story — one of love, fear, and loss. Parents often describe a swirl of conflicting emotions: guilt ("Did we miss something?"), fear ("Will they hate me for this?"), and grief ("This isn't the future I imagined for them — or for us"). These are not signs of weakness; they are signs of love. They emerge because something sacred — your sense of safety, predictability, and control — has been disrupted.

When a loved one or young adult begins to struggle, parents instinctively look inward for answers. It is human nature to scan the past for missteps: *If only we'd caught it sooner. If only we'd been stricter — or softer — or more available.* But guilt is a poor historian. It distorts memory through the lens of hindsight. In truth, most parents are doing their best with the information they have in real time. Addiction, depression, anxiety, trauma — these are not the result of moral failure or parental neglect. They are complex biopsychosocial conditions, shaped by genetics, environment, development, and circumstance.

Still, guilt persists because it gives the illusion of control. If we can blame ourselves, we can believe we could have prevented it. Letting go of that illusion means facing the harder truth: some things are simply beyond our power to prevent — but not beyond our power to influence.

Choosing Courage Over Control

Seeking higher care for your loved one is one of the most courageous acts of parenting there is. It goes against every instinct to protect by proximity — to keep them close, to manage every detail, to soothe the immediate distress. But real protection often looks different than imagined. It looks like surrendering control to structure, entrusting your loved one to a team of professionals, and admitting that love alone, though essential, is not enough to heal what requires specialized care.

It helps to remember: choosing treatment is not an admission of failure. It is an act of profound courage — choosing structure when chaos feels easier, truth over secrecy, and healing over optics. It means prioritizing wellness over appearances, and long-term safety over short-term comfort. Parents who make this choice are not "sending their loved one away." They are expanding the circle of care — inviting in others who can help hold what has become too heavy to carry alone.

In family therapy, it helps to remind parents:
"You're not sending your loved one away — you're expanding the circle of people who love them enough to help while providing a safe environment to heal."

That reframing matters, because it shifts the emotional stance from *abandonment* to *alignment.* It centers love in the decision, not loss.

The Emotional Layers: Guilt, Fear, and Grief

Guilt whispers that you should have done more. It points backward, searching for the moment when everything could have turned out differently. But guilt often masks grief — grief for the imagined story you once held: the milestones, the stability, the version of family life you thought would unfold. Naming that grief is essential. It allows you to mourn not only what has been lost but also what is changing.

Fear looks forward — it worries about outcomes. *Will they resent me? Will this work? What if things get worse before they get better?* Fear thrives in uncertainty, and treatment introduces a lot of it. The antidote to fear is faith — not blind optimism, but trust in the process, trust in the team, and trust in your capacity to endure discomfort for the sake of healing.

Grief weaves through every stage of the journey. It is the quiet ache of realizing that recovery does not follow a straight line, that your loved one's path may look different than you hoped. Grief is not weakness — it is the heart acknowledging reality. Allowing yourself to grieve is what creates space for compassion and flexibility, both essential to sustained family healing.

Bringing It All Together: The Arc of Recovery

Recovery is not a straight line. It rarely moves neatly from crisis to stability, from treatment to wellness. More often, it unfolds as a looping, adaptive process — a mix of progress, pauses, and revisiting old challenges in new ways. Families often describe it as two steps forward, one step back. But what looks like backtracking from the outside is often growth in disguise — a sign that the system is learning to adapt to stress rather than collapse under it.

In reality, most families move up and down the continuum of care over time. A teen or young adult might begin in outpatient therapy, progress to an intensive outpatient program (IOP), return to outpatient as things stabilize, and then re-engage in higher care during periods of relapse, transition, or emotional overwhelm. These shifts can be unsettling, but they are not signs of failure. They are signs of *responsiveness.* Recovery is a living process — dynamic, flexible, and deeply influenced by life's seasons.

The goal is not perfection. It is progression — a gradual widening of capacity, resilience, and self-awareness. Each step, even the backward ones, contributes to a deeper understanding of what wellness requires.

The Spiral Staircase of Healing

Imagine recovery as a spiral staircase rather than a straight ladder. From above, it may look like you're circling the same issues — communication, boundaries, trust, accountability — again and again. But if you look more closely, you'll see that each turn of the spiral brings you to a slightly higher vantage point. You're not back where you started; you're revisiting familiar terrain with more perspective, skill, and emotional endurance.

The first time your teen or young adult enters treatment, the family may be focused on crisis stabilization — safety, containment, and regulation. When treatment occurs again months or years later, the focus may shift to skill building or relapse prevention. A later phase might explore identity, purpose, or emotional depth. The themes repeat, but the learning evolves. Each turn of the spiral is another layer of integration — insight moving from head to heart to habit.

This spiral model also honors the truth that growth is cyclical, not linear. Life's stressors — transitions, losses, relationships — often reawaken old coping mechanisms. The difference over time is that the family learns to recognize and respond differently. The same triggers no longer generate the same chaos. That is progress — quiet, cumulative, and real.

From Crisis Management to Sustainable Change

In the early stages, recovery often feels like crisis management. Everyone's energy is directed toward preventing harm, de-escalating conflict, and stabilizing the home. The nervous system of the family runs hot — constant vigilance, emotional reactivity, exhaustion. Over time, as safety and structure return, families can begin to shift from reacting to *responding.*

This next stage — what clinicians call maintenance — isn't about relaxing vigilance; it is about redistributing it. Parents begin to trust the process, their loved one begins to trust themselves, and the system begins to breathe again. The focus moves from *putting out fires* to *learning fire prevention*: communication, boundary consistency, relapse planning, and emotional regulation.

True sustainability comes when recovery becomes integrated into daily life rather than treated as an emergency response. The family learns to identify early warning signs and respond with reflection rather than panic. They begin to talk openly about stress, accountability, and needs — not just when things fall apart, but as an ongoing rhythm of relationship.

The Role of Setbacks

Setbacks are part of the process, not proof of failure. They often occur at transitional points — moving from structured care back to independence, changing therapists, or navigating milestones like college or employment. Setbacks reveal where the system still needs reinforcement.

A relapse, for instance, does not erase progress; it exposes vulnerability. it is a message: *This area still needs more support.* In this sense, relapse can become data — feedback that refines treatment, not invalidates it. Families who approach setbacks with curiosity instead of catastrophe discover that each challenge strengthens their collective resilience.

In family therapy, we often use the phrase "relapse is information." It tells you where the coping system buckled, what stressor overwhelmed the available tools, and what kind of support might help next time. When framed this way, recovery stops being a test you can fail and becomes a lifelong practice you can refine.

Family Recovery: Parallel and Interwoven

Just as the individual in treatment learns to regulate emotions, tolerate distress, and rebuild trust, so too must the family. The two recoveries are parallel but deeply interwoven. Parents learn to set boundaries without collapsing into guilt, to communicate without criticism, and to stay connected without rescuing. Over time, these new relational patterns begin to shape the home environment into something more sustainable.

One parent described this beautifully:
"At first, I thought recovery was about my son getting sober. Then I realized it was about all of us learning how to live differently — how to stop walking on eggshells, how to speak honestly, how to breathe again."

When parents commit to their own healing — through therapy, support groups, or education — they reinforce the foundation beneath their loved one's growth. The family becomes not a trigger for relapse but a buffer against it.

Measuring Growth Over Time

Recovery can be hard to measure because its most meaningful changes are often invisible at first. The early milestones may be small: a calm conversation where shouting once erupted, a willingness to ask for help, a week of consistent sleep, a renewed sense of humor. Over months and years, these small shifts compound into something durable — emotional maturity, self-awareness, and reconnected relationships.

Progress may not always look dramatic, but it becomes deeply felt. Parents notice that they no longer wake each morning braced for crisis. Their loved one begins to take ownership of routines, communicate needs, and rebuild trust through consistency rather than promises. The atmosphere in the home changes — from tension to tentative safety, from survival to genuine connection.

These are the true markers of healing: not the absence of struggle, but the presence of resilience.

The Long View

The arc of recovery is best understood not as a destination, but as a practice — a way of living that prioritizes awareness, honesty, and growth. The families who thrive long-term are not the ones who never face setbacks, but the ones who learn how to recover from them faster, with less shame and more collaboration.

Progress is measured not in perfection but in pace — how quickly repair follows rupture, how often honesty replaces secrecy, how consistently communication replaces conflict. Each turn of the spiral brings the family closer to balance.

If recovery has an endpoint, it is this: a renewed ability to live in truth. To acknowledge what is hard, to celebrate what is working, and to trust that healing can continue even when the path curves.

Reflection Exercise: Mapping Your Family's Next Step

1. Where does my loved one currently fall on the continuum of care?
2. Which option feels most aligned with their current needs, not just my comfort?

3. What fears come up when I picture increasing structure?
4. What would relief look like if the right support were in place?
5. What is one step I can take this week — a call, a consultation, a conversation — toward clarity?

Write your answers down. Patterns often emerge when you see them on paper.

Chapter 8

Healing the Parent While the Loved One

> **You can't pour from an empty cup — and you can't guide someone through healing while refusing your own**

When a loved one enters treatment or begins recovery, parents often exhale for the first time in months. The crisis feels momentarily contained. But then a new kind of ache sets in — a silence filled with exhaustion, confusion, and unspoken grief. Parents describe this stage as "standing still while everything keeps moving." Their loved one is in therapy, learning new language and tools, while they're left managing the daily rhythm of uncertainty. The focus remains on the young person's progress, but the parent's healing is equally vital.

The truth is simple and profound: recovery is relational. Families heal together, or they struggle in parallel silence.

Understanding the Parallel Process

The term *parallel process* comes from family systems theory, a framework that views families not as collections of individuals but as interconnected emotional ecosystems. In this view, what happens to one member inevitably affects the others. The system is always seeking balance — sometimes healthy, sometimes not — and any change within it, however small, sends ripples through the whole. This is why recovery cannot be the work of one person alone. When one member of the family begins to change — to regulate emotions, take responsibility, communicate differently, or assert boundaries — the entire system must adapt in response.

In the context of recovery, this dynamic becomes both the challenge and the opportunity for transformation. When a young person begins to heal — to step into ownership, honesty, and accountability — the parent is also called to change. If that does not happen, if the family unconsciously clings to familiar emotional roles, even well-intentioned love can pull everyone back into chaos. For example, if the young person starts to take ownership of their choices but the parent continues to over-manage out of fear, the system quietly reinforces dependence. If the young person practices vulnerability but the parent responds with judgment or panic, openness becomes unsafe again. Without parallel growth, old patterns reassert themselves — not because anyone failed, but because systems instinctively return to what's familiar.

When a loved one learns to take ownership, the parent must learn to release control. This does not mean withdrawing support; it means shifting from command to collaboration, from rescuing to respecting. Parents who have spent months or years managing crises often feel unsteady when they're no longer needed in the same way. Yet this letting go is an act of faith — trusting that the skills being built in treatment can begin to stand on their own. It allows the young person to experience true accountability and the parent to rediscover their own boundaries and identity beyond constant vigilance. When a loved one learns vulnerability, the parent must learn acceptance. As the young person begins to name emotions honestly — fear, shame, sadness, anger — the parent's task becomes holding space rather than fixing. It is natural to want to reassure or correct, to say "Don't think that way," or "You're stronger than that." But what helps most is the quiet presence that says, *I can sit with you in this.* Acceptance transforms vulnerability from a liability into a bridge — one that reconnects the relationship through authenticity and empathy. And when a loved one learns boundaries, the parent must learn trust. Recovery often teaches young people to identify what's healthy for them

— to ask for privacy, space, or time. These new limits can feel like rejection to a parent accustomed to constant access. Trust means recognizing that healthy distance is part of connection, not a threat to it. It is allowing the relationship to mature alongside the person's healing, to move from supervision to mutual respect.

The parallel process reminds us that recovery is not a solo act. Healing that occurs in isolation — one person changing while the rest of the system remains the same — is actually not possible. The most enduring transformations happen when everyone in the family evolves together, each learning their own version of regulation, communication, and accountability. it is not about doing identical work, but about doing complementary work. The young person learns to take responsibility for themselves; the parent learns to release control. The young person learns honesty and openness; the parent learns to respond with steadiness and compassion. The young person practices boundaries; the parent practices trust.

In this way, healing becomes mutual, not one-directional. It is a dance of adjustment — messy, sometimes uncomfortable, but profoundly human. When parents and loved one grow in parallel, each person's progress reinforces the other's. The relationship shifts from one built on crisis management to one built on connection, respect, and shared growth.

Ultimately, the parallel process is what makes recovery sustainable. Without it, progress is temporary — easily undone by the gravitational pull of old dynamics. But when families embrace the truth that healing belongs to everyone, not just the identified client, the system stabilizes. New patterns emerge: less reactivity, more reflection; less control, more collaboration. What once felt like chaos begins to feel like movement — the family evolving together, learning not just to survive recovery, but to grow through it.

Grief, Guilt, and Growth

Most parents who walk the path of a loved one's recovery carry three invisible weights: grief, guilt, and vigilance. They may not speak of them aloud, but these emotions shape nearly every thought, every interaction, and every decision. They form the undercurrent of a parent's internal world — the quiet hum that persists long after the crisis has passed.

There is grief for the loved one who once laughed easily, who came home on time, who seemed safe in the world — or for the future that once felt certain. Many parents describe mourning not only what has been lost, but also what might never unfold in the way they imagined. There is a unique heartbreak in watching a loved one suffer and realizing that love cannot immediately restore what's been broken. This kind of grief is ambiguous: the person you love is still here, but something essential feels changed. You are both grieving the past and fearing what may come, caught in the space between memory and hope.

Then there is guilt — the most persistent and punishing of emotions. Parents replay the past, scanning for missed signs and second chances. *Should I have intervened sooner? Was I too strict? Too lenient? Too trusting?* This self-interrogation offers a painful illusion of control: if I caused it, maybe I can undo it. But guilt distorts perspective. It erases context and overestimates power. In truth, no parent has full visibility into the inner world of their loved one — especially when that loved one is struggling with the secrecy, shame, and complexity that accompany substance use or mental health challenges. Guilt, though understandable, can become a form of self-punishment that blocks empathy, both for yourself and your loved one.

Additionally, there is vigilance. Even after stability returns, many parents live in a state of quiet readiness — scanning for signs of relapse, regression, or danger. Sleep becomes light; joy becomes tentative. The nervous system stays braced for the next phone call, the next emergency, the next disappointment. This vigilance is born of love and trauma intertwined. It reflects both the memory of crisis and the terror of its return. Yet constant hyper-alertness can erode connection. It keeps the family emotionally suspended in the past, reacting to ghosts rather than realities.

These emotions — grief, guilt, vigilance — are normal and universal among families navigating recovery. They are not evidence of failure; they are evidence of care. But when they remain unacknowledged or unexpressed, they harden into barriers. Guilt can morph into overprotection, making parents micromanage or rescue out of fear. Grief can lead to withdrawal, a kind of emotional distance born from self-preservation. Vigilance can turn into mistrust, where love feels indistinguishable from surveillance. These patterns, while understandable, often recreate the very disconnection that everyone is trying to heal.

Healing begins with permission — the permission to feel everything, without judgment or apology. You can love your loved one and still feel angry. You can be grateful they're safe and still grieve the years lost to chaos. You can be hopeful and exhausted in the same breath. Both are true. Recovery asks for this kind of emotional flexibility — the capacity to hold multiple truths at once. It invites parents to move from *either/or* thinking to *both/and* understanding. In family therapy, this is often the turning point: when parents stop editing their emotions and start naming them. *"I'm so relieved she's sober, and I'm also terrified it won't last." "I'm proud of how far he's come, and I still feel angry about what happened."* Naming does not make these feelings disappear, but it prevents them from festering in silence. Once spoken, they can be understood, shared, and integrated.

Grief softens when it is witnessed. Guilt loosens when it is met with compassion. Vigilance eases when trust begins to rebuild. The paradox of recovery is that growth emerges not by suppressing emotion, but by allowing it. Each feeling, once acknowledged, becomes information — a signal pointing toward what still needs care.

For some parents, growth begins quietly: a deeper breath, a night of uninterrupted sleep, a moment of laughter that does not feel disloyal to the pain that came before. For others, it begins through connection — joining a support group, starting therapy, or speaking honestly with a friend who understands. Healing rarely arrives in a dramatic revelation; it arrives in small, consistent acts of truth-telling.

Over time, these emotions — grief, guilt, vigilance — begin to transform. Grief evolves into gratitude for what still remains. Guilt becomes humility, a gentler awareness that no parent can control the trajectory of another person's life. Vigilance becomes attentiveness — a capacity to stay aware without staying afraid.

This is the hidden alchemy of recovery. Pain, when met with honesty and compassion, becomes wisdom. Fear, when softened by trust, becomes awareness. And grief becomes love in its most resilient form. You do not need to banish these emotions to heal. You only need to make space for them — to let them live alongside hope. Because in the end, it is not about erasing the past; it is about integrating it into a story where both suffering and strength have a place.

The Role of Self-Compassion

In nearly every family navigating a loved one's recovery, the person who receives the least compassion is often the parent. From the outside, parents are expected to be pillars — steady, unshakable, endlessly supportive. They are told to be strong, to hold boundaries, to stay calm, to lead by example. And while these qualities are essential, they can easily harden into self-denial. Strength without softness becomes rigidity; resolve without gentleness becomes depletion. Over time, parents can lose touch with their own emotional needs, mistaking endurance for resilience.

In the whirlwind of treatment decisions, late-night fears, and constant uncertainty, it is easy for parents to forget that they, too, are human. They, too, are grieving, learning, and adjusting. Self-compassion does not mean self-pity or resignation. It means recognizing your own suffering and responding to it with the same care you would offer your loved one. It is not indulgent — it is restorative. It refuels the very system that holds the family together.

In therapy, I often see parents speak about themselves in ways they would never speak to anyone else. They say things like, *"I should have known better." "I can't believe I let it get this far." "If I were stronger, maybe they wouldn't be struggling."* These are the voices of exhaustion and guilt, not truth. When parents shift that inner dialogue toward compassion, everything begins to soften. The nervous system calms, perspective widens, and the capacity to stay emotionally available increases.

Self-compassion begins with awareness — noticing how you speak to yourself in moments of fear or frustration. Would you want to talk to your loved one the way you talk to yourself? If your loved one came to you in pain, would you want to respond with shame or accusation or would you prefer reassurance, patience, and understanding? The invitation is to extend that same care inward. Try saying to yourself, *"You're learning." "it is okay to be tired." "You deserve support, too."* These may seem like small phrases, but they are powerful counterweights to self-criticism. They interrupt the cycle of blame and replace it with belonging. Research in compassion-focused therapy and mindfulness shows that self-compassion activates the body's soothing system, reducing cortisol and increasing emotional regulation. In plain terms: when you are kind to yourself, you think more clearly, react less impulsively, and recover from stress faster. For parents in recovery families, this is vital. Your calmness is not only for you — it is the emotional anchor your loved one unconsciously relies on. Self-compassion replenishes the oxygen you need to keep breathing through uncertainty.

It also redefines what strength means. Many parents equate strength with stoicism — with holding everything together no matter how much it hurts. But real strength is flexible; it allows for tears, vulnerability, and rest. Self-compassion says, *"I can be scared and capable at the same time."* It acknowledges fatigue without judgment and makes space for renewal. Without it, even the most devoted parent risks burning out — physically, emotionally, and spiritually.

Self-compassion is also an act of modeling. When your loved one witnesses you offering yourself grace instead of punishment, they learn that recovery is not about perfection but persistence. They see that being human — making mistakes, struggling, starting again — is not something to hide but something to honor. In this way, your self-care becomes their template for resilience. There is a quiet dignity in parents who practice compassion toward themselves. They do not stop feeling fear or sadness, but they stop fighting themselves for feeling it. They begin to understand that the same empathy they extend to their loved one belongs to them, too. And as they nurture that gentleness, they discover a new kind of steadiness — one rooted not in control, but in kindness.

Self-compassion creates emotional oxygen — the kind that keeps you grounded through setbacks, centered during conflict, and openhearted through uncertainty. It allows you to show up not as a perfect parent, but as a present one. And in the long arc of recovery, that presence — imperfect, consistent, human — is what heals families more than anything else.

The Systemic Ripple

Family systems are living organisms. Every member is connected through invisible threads of emotion, history, and habit. When one person changes — truly changes — the entire system feels it. In families navigating recovery, this often begins with the parent. The moment a parent starts to heal, something subtle but powerful happens: the emotional temperature in the home begins to shift.

Parents are the emotional barometers of the family. When they are tense, the atmosphere tightens; when they soften, the air becomes breathable again. Healing does not require perfection — it begins with small moments of awareness and regulation. A parent who takes a mindful breath before reacting to conflict sends an unspoken message: *We can do this differently.* Over time, that single act ripples outward. Siblings feel less invisible. The household feels less like a pressure chamber. The young person in recovery senses the difference — less scrutiny, more space, less fear, more possibility. Loved ones, especially those in recovery, are exquisitely attuned to emotional tone. They may not respond to words, but they respond to energy. When parents shift from anxious control to calm presence, from frantic problem-solving to grounded listening, the nervous system of the entire family begins to settle. The home becomes less about managing crisis and more about cultivating safety. This does not mean the road ahead is smooth — but it means the family can walk it with steadier footing.

Healing is rarely linear, but it is deeply contagious. Calm begets calm. When a parent begins therapy, sets boundaries, or practices self-compassion, it models resilience. The parent's regulation becomes the family's anchor. As the parent's nervous system finds stability, everyone else's system adjusts in kind. The siblings stop bracing for conflict. The partner exhales. The young person feels less like the center of the storm and more like part of a family that is learning together. This is the quiet magic of systemic healing: one person's growth becomes the family's growth. The calmer the parent, the safer the family feels. The safer the family, the stronger the recovery. Stability is not built through control but through consistency — through a parent's steady ability to remain present, compassionate, and curious even when things are uncertain.

In time, this shift creates a new kind of homeostasis — not the old fragile balance held together by anxiety, but a deeper, truer balance grounded in openness, trust, and connection. Recovery becomes less about rules and more about relationships. It becomes less about avoiding relapse and more about cultivating resilience. And it all begins with one person's willingness to turn inward, to heal, and to model what calm courage looks like in real life.

When parents begin to heal, the family no longer orbits around fear — it begins to orbit around hope.

Types of Resources Available for Parents

Family recovery does not end when a loved one enters treatment. In many ways, it is just beginning. While clinicians focus on helping the adolescent or young adult stabilize, parents have their own work to do — learning new patterns, processing emotions, and developing resilience. This is known as the *parallel process*: as your loved one heals, you heal alongside them. The tools and support systems that sustain this journey are as essential as any treatment plan.

Individual Therapy

Personal therapy gives parents a private space to explore the complex emotions that accompany their loved one's struggle — fear, guilt, grief, anger, exhaustion. It allows for honest reflection without the pressure to stay strong or have all the answers. Therapists who specialize in family systems, trauma, or substance use can help parents understand their roles in the dynamic and develop healthier responses to stress. Over time, this work strengthens boundaries, improves communication, and helps parents reclaim their sense of identity beyond crisis management. Therapy isn't just for the loved one in treatment; it is a lifeline for the parent, too.

Parent Coaching

Parent coaching bridges the gap between therapy and everyday life. Coaches, often clinicians with specialized training in family recovery, provide practical tools and real-time guidance. Sessions might focus on communication scripts, boundary setting, emotional regulation, or navigating treatment systems. Coaching is action-oriented — helping parents translate insight into behavior change. Many parents find that coaching gives them structure and accountability during a time when everything feels uncertain. It offers a roadmap for responding to difficult situations without losing connection or clarity.

Support Groups for Parents

No parent should walk this path alone. Groups like Al-Anon, Nar-Anon, SMART Recovery Family & Friends, and Parent Coaching Alliance create safe spaces for sharing experiences, learning from others, and releasing shame. Hearing another parent say, "I've been there," can be profoundly healing. Support groups normalize the chaos and isolation of loving someone with addiction or mental-health challenges. They also offer perspective — helping parents distinguish between what they can control and what they can't. Whether in person or online, group support fosters connection, which is an antidote to shame and burnout.

Family Therapy

Parallel process work deepens when the whole family is included. Family therapy focuses on the interactions and patterns that shape recovery: communication styles, boundary maintenance, emotional safety, and trust repair. It is not about assigning blame; it is about restoring balance. A skilled family therapist helps parents and loved ones hear one another differently, creating space for empathy and accountability on both sides. Over time, this shared work rebuilds the emotional scaffolding that supports long-term healing.

Educational and Psychoeducational Resources

Knowledge reduces fear. Workshops, webinars, and family education programs offered by treatment centers or community organizations teach the science behind addiction, mental health, trauma, and recovery. Understanding the neurobiology of stress, for example, can help parents interpret behavior with compassion rather than reactivity. These programs also introduce practical frameworks for parenting through crisis, regulating emotions, and supporting post-treatment reintegration. Many families find that education transforms helplessness into informed confidence.

Peer Mentorship and Recovery Communities

Some organizations connect parents with trained mentors — other parents who have been through similar experiences. These relationships offer a rare kind of empathy: the wisdom of someone who truly understands the fear, the waiting, and the work. Community-based initiatives, recovery networks, and online forums can provide accessible, nonjudgmental support between formal sessions. In the same way that peer recovery coaches guide individuals in sobriety, parent mentors can model emotional regulation, hope, and perseverance.

Faith and Mindfulness-Based Support

For some, spirituality or mindfulness offers grounding that therapy alone cannot. Practices like meditation, journaling, yoga, or contemplative prayer help parents regulate their nervous systems and reconnect with meaning. These practices don't replace professional help but complement it — creating moments of quiet where insight and compassion can take root. Parents often report that mindfulness helps them respond to crises with more clarity and less fear, reinforcing their ability to lead calmly through turbulence.

Reflection & Practice

1. **List three things you've lost during your loved one's struggle.** Then list three things you've gained — even if they're small, like perspective or patience.
2. **Ask yourself:** What does my nervous system need today — rest, connection, movement, or quiet? Give it 10 minutes.
3. **Notice patterns of guilt.** When it arises, pause and reframe: *Guilt means I care. But I can care without punishment.*

4. **Create one ritual just for yourself.** A walk, journaling, a weekly coffee — something that belongs only to your recovery.

Chapter 9

Recovery Is a Family Affair

> *Recovery does not mean life goes back to what it was. It means we learn how to live—together—in a new way*

By the time most families reach stability, they have weathered storms that once seemed impossible. The emergencies quiet down. The calls in the night grow fewer. There are still tense moments, but laughter starts to return. The air feels lighter.

And then a new question arises: *Now what?*

Recovery, at its core, isn't about returning to the old normal. It is about building something wiser, gentler, and more connected than what existed before.

From Individual Work to Collective Healing

In the early stages of recovery, the focus often centers on the individual — the adolescent or young adult learning new coping skills, practicing sobriety, attending therapy sessions, and rebuilding trust in themselves. The family rallies around them, monitoring progress, adjusting schedules, and holding collective breath with every small step forward. But over time, many families come to a vital realization: true recovery cannot rest on the shoulders of one person. The healing of one member depends on the health of the entire system. The family's growth — its ability to communicate, regulate emotion, and create safety — becomes just as essential as the individual's progress.

Healing, then, evolves into a shared ecosystem rather than an isolated project. Parents begin to do their own emotional work — learning to regulate anxiety before reacting, to speak with calm rather than fear, and to listen for meaning beneath behavior. Siblings, who may have felt overlooked during the chaos of a crisis, start finding their voices again. They learn that their feelings matter, that they are not defined by the illness or recovery of their brother or sister. Partners learn to reconnect as a team rather than as co-managers of a crisis. Slowly, the household tone begins to shift: less reactivity, more reflection; less blame, more belonging.

As each member begins to grow, the family transforms from a set of separate coping mechanisms into a living network of mutual support. Parents model emotional regulation, showing that anger and love can coexist. Siblings learn that they can express disappointment or fear without destabilizing the family. The loved one in recovery feels this shift most powerfully — the environment becomes less charged, less defined by tension and control, and more rooted in trust and possibility. Recovery stops being something *done to* one person and becomes something *shared among* all.

This movement from individual work to collective healing is what turns recovery into resilience. Families that learn to regulate together communicate differently, handle setbacks with more stability, and find new rhythms of connection. They begin to measure progress not only by abstinence or symptom reduction, but by relational markers: honest conversations, laughter returning to the home, moments of genuine peace. When every member participates, healing becomes the family's new language — one spoken through presence, compassion, and accountability.

When recovery becomes collective, wellness becomes culture.

The Family as a Recovery Environment

A supportive family does not mean one without conflict or imperfection. Rather, it means a family that learns to approach conflict with respect, repair, and reflection instead of blame or avoidance. In recovery, the home becomes more than a place to live — it becomes a living environment that teaches emotional safety, accountability, and resilience. When families learn to handle rupture and repair skillfully, the atmosphere shifts from one of tension and reactivity to one of stability and trust. The home transforms into a space where honesty is met with empathy, not panic — where truth no longer threatens connection, but strengthens it.

Families that thrive in recovery share certain habits that create this environment of safety and growth. Predictability is one of them. Consistent routines — mealtimes, check-ins, curfews, daily rituals — help reduce anxiety and reactivity. Predictability does not eliminate emotion, but it gives it structure. For a young person whose nervous system has been shaped by chaos, knowing what to expect helps them begin to relax. Transparency is another cornerstone. Secrets shrink in the light of open dialogue. Families who name what's happening — who say, "This is hard for all of us, and we're figuring it out together" — model courage and honesty, replacing the old cycle of secrecy and shame with openness and collaboration.

Then there is repair — the skill that turns conflict into connection. Every family argues, especially in recovery, but what matters is what happens afterward. Repair means someone steps forward quickly to take responsibility: "I lost my temper — can we try again?" it is not about being right; it is about restoring trust. This small act signals emotional maturity and keeps relationships intact even when emotions run high. Over time, repair teaches everyone in the household that rupture is not the end of connection — it is an opportunity for reconnection.

Lastly, recovery-oriented families practice shared accountability. In these households, there is no "identified patient." Everyone has work to do. The young person learns coping and honesty; parents learn boundaries and regulation; siblings learn self-expression and empathy. This collective accountability dismantles the old hierarchy of "the problem loved one" and replaces it with a culture of mutual growth. When each member owns their part, shame begins to dissolve and authenticity takes its place.

These habits — predictability, transparency, repair, and shared accountability — slowly rewire the nervous system of the household. What was once a landscape of hypervigilance and fear becomes one of steadiness and safety. Parents stop reacting from panic; loved ones stop guarding against judgment. The family learns, together, that love can hold boundaries and that connection can coexist with accountability. In this kind of home, recovery does not feel like punishment — it feels like belonging.

Redefining Success

For many parents, success in recovery has been defined by a single, measurable goal: abstinence. The logic seems simple — if their teen or young adult isn't in active addiction, everything must be okay. But over time, most families discover that this narrow definition overlooks the deeper work of healing. True recovery is not just the absence of use; it is the presence of growth — the ability to live with honesty, emotional awareness, connection, and resilience. Sobriety matters, of course, but it is not the full story. A young person can be abstinent and still disconnected, anxious, or shut down. The real goal is a life that feels meaningful and self-directed — one that is not merely free of addiction, but full of integrity and purpose.

When parents begin to see recovery as a process rather than a finish line, their perspective shifts from control to curiosity. Relapse, mood swings, and setbacks stop being treated as evidence of failure and start being understood as information. These moments reveal where more healing is needed — where the system is still tender, or where old coping strategies resurface under stress. The focus moves from punishment to understanding. Instead of asking, *"Why did this happen again?"* families begin to ask, *"What is this moment teaching us?"* This shift reframes relapse or regression not as a collapse of progress, but as a signal that deeper support or reflection is required. In long-term recovery, families learn that progress looks different than they imagined. It is not measured in clean weeks or perfect days; it is measured in repair and resilience — in how quickly trust can be rebuilt after a rupture, in how openly feelings are shared, in how safely each person can be honest without fear of rejection. A difficult truth spoken calmly, a moment of accountability accepted without defensiveness, or a night when an argument ends in understanding instead of silence — these are the milestones that mark real change.

Redefining success also means releasing the illusion of a linear journey. Recovery does not unfold like a staircase; it moves like a tide — advancing, retreating, finding its rhythm. Families who learn to ride these waves with steadiness, rather than panic, cultivate a new kind of strength. They stop expecting perfection and start celebrating repair — the courage to come back together after conflict, to recommit after disappointment, to keep choosing connection even when the path is uneven. Over time, this new definition of success reshapes the family's emotional landscape. The home no longer feels like a testing ground where worth is measured by outcomes. It becomes a sanctuary of learning, where growth is valued over performance and compassion outweighs judgment. Parents begin to see their role not as monitors of behavior, but as stewards of relationship — guiding, modeling, and believing in the possibility of transformation even when progress feels slow.

Ultimately, success in recovery is not about achieving flawlessness. It is about cultivating truth, safety, and endurance — the capacity to keep moving forward together, even when the way is uncertain. Every time honesty replaces shame, every time connection survives struggle, recovery deepens. The family learns that healing is not a single victory but a lifelong practice — one that turns set-backs into wisdom and love into lasting strength.

Sustaining the Work

Recovery does not end when the crisis subsides or when formal treatment concludes. In many ways, that is where the true work begins. Maintaining recovery — both for the individual and the family — is less about perfection and more about consistent tending, much like caring for a garden. It requires ongoing attention, gentle structure, and the willingness to pull weeds before they overtake new growth. The garden metaphor captures the truth of long-term healing: progress flourishes when nurtured, but old patterns — resentment, avoidance, fear, or control — will always try to return if left unattended. Sustaining recovery is about noticing those weeds early and choosing, again and again, to cultivate connection and care.

Healthy families in long-term recovery develop rhythms that support ongoing reflection and communication. Regular check-ins become one of the most effective tools. Some families schedule weekly meetings, brief and structured, where each person can share what's working and what feels hard. Others keep shared journals, leaving notes of gratitude, apology, or encouragement for one another. These small rituals of dialogue prevent misunderstandings from festering and remind everyone that communication is a practice, not an emergency response. Over time, these consistent moments of honesty replace reactive conversations with intentional ones, allowing the family to stay connected even when emotions run high.

Shared wellness practices also help sustain the emotional foundation of recovery. Families who walk together after dinner, cook meals side by side, or pause each day to name what they're grateful for often find that healing deepens through routine acts of presence. These practices are not about forced togetherness but about relearning how to coexist in calm. They rebuild safety through simple, repeatable experiences that ground the body and spirit. For a family once accustomed to chaos, these quiet moments of shared activity communicate a powerful message: *We can be peaceful together.*

Another cornerstone of sustained recovery is community connection. Families that continue participating in therapy, peer support groups, or spiritual and creative communities tend to maintain progress more effectively than those who try to go it alone. Whether it is ongoing family therapy, Al-Anon, Nar-Anon, or a local recovery network, these spaces offer accountability and encouragement. They remind parents that relapse, fear, or fatigue are not signs of failure but signals that more care is needed. In recovery, community functions as a mirror — reflecting back your strength when you forget you have it.

Celebrating progress is another vital part of sustaining the work. In the same way that gardeners mark the seasons, families can honor milestones — sobriety anniversaries, improved grades, honest conversations, moments of self-awareness. These celebrations need not be elaborate; what matters is recognition. A simple "I noticed how calmly you handled that" or "I'm proud of how we got through that argument together" reinforces the belief that growth is happening, even in small ways. These acknowledgments keep motivation alive and shift focus from what's wrong to what's working.

Ultimately, sustaining recovery means moving from crisis prevention to growth cultivation. Early recovery is about survival — managing risk, containing chaos, keeping everyone safe. Long-term recovery is about expansion — building meaning, deepening connection, and learning to live with curiosity rather than fear. Families who reach this stage understand that maintenance is not static; it is dynamic. It evolves with each season of life, requiring continued awareness and adaptability.

When a family tends to recover the way a gardener tends to soil — with patience, attention, and reverence for the process — healing becomes part of everyday life. The home no longer feels defined by what was lost, but by what continues to grow. And in that ongoing care, families discover that recovery isn't just something they maintain — it is something they live.

The Role of Hope

Hope is the quiet engine of family recovery — the invisible current that keeps movement possible even when the waters are rough. It is not naïve or blind optimism; it is not pretending everything is fine when it isn't. True hope is far more courageous than that. It is the deliberate decision to believe in possibility *even after disappointment*. It is what allows a parent to get up each morning and keep showing up for their loved one, even when progress feels fragile or setbacks appear without warning. Hope says, *we are not finished yet.*

In families navigating substance use and mental health challenges, hope becomes both anchor and compass. It grounds you in the belief that healing is possible and guides you toward the next right action when the future feels uncertain. Parents who learn to hold hope not as an outcome but as a *stance* model something profoundly powerful to their loved ones: resilience. Teens and young adults who have stumbled — who carry shame, regret, or self-doubt — often cannot yet imagine a future in which they are trusted, stable, or well. They borrow hope from those around them. A parent's steady, quiet faith in their capacity to grow becomes a bridge across despair. Hope, in this sense, is not a feeling but a *transmission* — one nervous system whispering to another, *you are not beyond repair.*

A father who captured this truth beautifully reported that after years of crisis, therapy, and exhaustion, he said, "I learned that hope isn't expecting everything to be perfect — it is trusting that we can handle whatever comes." His words revealed the essence of sustainable hope. It is not about controlling outcomes or erasing pain. It is about building confidence in your family's ability to navigate what arises. That shift — from needing things to be okay to trusting you can face them even when they're not — is what transforms survival into resilience.

Families who live with this kind of hope develop quieter nervous systems. Fear no longer dictates every reaction. They begin to interpret setbacks not as signs of failure but as reminders to realign, reconnect, and recalibrate. Hope does not deny pain; it contextualizes it. It reminds parents and loved ones alike that healing is not linear, but forward motion is still possible even when it feels slow. Each honest conversation, each moment of regulation after conflict, each boundary held with compassion is evidence that growth is happening — proof that life after chaos is being built, brick by brick.

Over time, hope reshapes the emotional landscape of the family. It replaces hypervigilance with perspective, shame with self-compassion, and fear with faith in the process. it is the light that keeps parents walking when the path grows dim and the force that draws young people back toward connection after relapse or withdrawal. Hope transforms the narrative from *What if it all falls apart again?* To *even if it does, we know how to rebuild.*

Ultimately, hope is what allows families not just to recover, but to thrive. it is what turns endurance into evolution. When parents model hope — grounded, patient, realistic — they offer their loved one a living example of what healing looks like in motion: not perfection, but persistence; not certainty, but courage. Hope says, *We can do hard things, and we can do them together.* And that belief, quietly practiced over time, becomes the foundation on which recovery endures.

Reflection & Practice

1. **Family Gratitude Practice:** Each week, name one thing you appreciate about each other—something small but specific.
2. **Create a Recovery Ritual:** Light a candle at dinner, take a Sunday walk, or start a shared playlist. Symbols make progress visible.
3. **Check Your Language:** Replace "You need to…" with "How can we…" in daily conversation.
4. **Look Forward:** Write a family vision statement for the next year—what healing looks and feels like, not just what you want to avoid.

A Family's Journey Forward

Every family that steps into the landscape of recovery begins in a place of uncertainty. No one is ever fully prepared for what it asks — the patience, the honesty, the courage to look within as much as outward. Most parents begin by searching for answers about their loved one: *What will help? What went wrong? What should we do next?* But somewhere along the way, the questions shift. Recovery invites the family to ask not only *How can we fix this?* but *How can we heal together?* That is the essence of the family journey. It is not a straight path, and it does not unfold on anyone's preferred timeline. There will be calm seasons and stormy ones, moments of clarity followed by confusion. But through it all, families learn that healing is not defined by control, by certainty, or even by outcomes. It is defined by connection — by the ability to stay present, compassionate, and curious even when things are uncertain.

Along this path, parents begin to reclaim themselves. They rediscover their own voice after years of speaking through worry. They learn to breathe before reacting, to listen before fixing, to love without losing themselves. They realize that boundaries are not walls but bridges — structures that hold safety and respect on both sides. They learn that self-compassion is not weakness but strength, the very fuel that allows them to keep showing up with steadiness.

Siblings and partners, too, find their footing in this new ecosystem. They learn that they are part of the healing, not spectators to it. They begin to see that when one member grows, everyone grows. And as the family steadies itself, the young person in recovery begins to feel that stability, often before they can articulate it. The home that once felt like a battlefield starts to feel like a safe landing place again — not perfect, but real, and grounded in love that does not shatter under strain. This is what lasting recovery looks like: not the absence of struggle, but the presence of repair. Families learn to navigate conflict without collapse, to name pain without blame, and to celebrate progress in its many forms — an honest conversation, a calm night, a new boundary held with compassion. The extraordinary truth is that every one of these small moments matters. Together, they build the scaffolding of trust, the architecture of resilience that sustains recovery through the long arc of life.

Hope, as this journey reveals, is not about waiting for the storm to end — it is about learning how to stand together in the rain. Families that heal discover that hope is not a fragile thing; it is a practice, a discipline, a daily act of faith. it is the voice that says, *We can keep going. We can face this. We can grow.* And over time, that belief reshapes everything: how you speak, how you listen, how you love.

If there is one truth to carry forward, it is this: recovery is not a destination. It is a relationship — with your loved one, with your family, and with yourself. It evolves, it deepens, it stretches you in ways you never expected. But it also brings you home — to a place of honesty, compassion, and connection.

The work continues, as all meaningful work does. But the family who once lived in crisis now lives in consciousness — aware, connected, and alive to possibility. And that, more than anything else, is what healing truly means.

A Final Letter to Parents

Dear Parent,

If you have made it to this final page, I want you to pause for a moment.

Take a breath.

Because the very fact that you are here tells me something important about you - You care deeply. You are still showing up.

And despite the fear, frustration, exhaustion, and uncertainty — you have not stopped loving and showing up for your teen or young adult.

That matters more than you realize.

Parenting an adolescent or young adult who is struggling with substance use or mental health challenges can feel destabilizing. It can shake your confidence. It can strain your relationships. It can test your patience in ways you never imagined. You may have questioned your decisions. You may have replayed moments from years ago, wondering what you could have done differently.

Let me say this clearly: This is not about blame.

Throughout this book, I have asked you to shift from reacting out of fear to responding with intention. To move from controlling outcomes to strengthening your position. To replace chaos with clarity. To stop chasing your child's behavior and begin anchoring yourself.

That shift is not easy. It is uncomfortable. It requires restraint when everything inside you wants to escalate. It requires consistency when you are tired. It requires courage when the stakes feel high.

But it is possible.

Recovery and healing — for your loved one and for your family — is rarely linear. There will be progress and setbacks. There may be moments of hope followed by moments of disappointment. Do not let temporary turbulence convince you that change is impossible.

Sustainable change happens when the system shifts.

When you regulate before responding.
When you implement boundaries with calm consistency.
When you allow natural consequences to do their work.
When you engage in your own growth alongside your loved one's.

You do not need to be perfect.
You need to be steady.

Your loved one does not need a flawless parent.
They need a grounded one.

There will be days when fear gets loud. When you question whether you are doing enough — or doing too much. On those days, return to this: modeling and alignment over control. Stability over reactivity. Connection over chaos.

And remember that you are not meant to do this alone.

Seek support. Ask for guidance. Surround yourself with people who understand this work. Strong families are not the ones who avoid struggle — they are the ones who learn how to face it together.

If this book has offered even a small measure of clarity, relief, or direction, then it has served its purpose.

And when the path feels dark, remember — you are capable of being the light your family needs.

With respect and confidence in you,
Ben

About The Author

Ben Mushlin, LCSW

Ben's path to becoming a psychotherapist began with his own journey of healing from years of substance use, personal turmoil, and struggles with trauma. He was fortunate to receive selfless support from others along the way, which guided him toward hope, happiness, and a sense of freedom. Inspired by the transformative impact of those who helped him, Ben dedicated his life to offering the same guidance and compassion to others.

Before becoming a psychotherapist, Ben worked extensively in the field of substance use recovery across New York City, beginning in sober living residences and progressing to roles as a Recovery Coach and Case Manager. His passion for helping others deepened as he led a New York City Department of Health opioid overdose response team. Ben went on to pursue a Master of Social

Work degree at the Silberman School of Social Work at Hunter College. After completing his social work training, he practiced as a psychotherapist in an outpatient substance use treatment program and later became the director of a transitional living program for adults with co-occurring disorders. Before founding Searchlight Therapy, he served as Clinical Director at a premier outpatient treatment program in New York City, specializing in the treatment of adolescents, young adults, and their families.

Ben's approach is relational, compassionate, and deeply collaborative. He integrates evidence-based modalities—including cognitive-behavioral therapy (CBT), dialectical behavior therapy (DBT), motivational interviewing (MI), and family systems frameworks—with an emphasis on communication, resilience, and personal agency. His work centers on helping young people and their families move from crisis to connection, building sustainable tools for growth and recovery.

Ben founded Searchlight Therapy to have a space for adolescents, young adults, and their families to receive high quality, compassionate, and customizable substance use and co-occurring mental health disorder treatment. Drawing on years of experience in both clinical treatment and family systems work, Ben has built Searchlight Therapy around a central philosophy: *healing happens when the whole family is engaged, supported, and illuminated by understanding.*